A Dutch Heritage
200 Years of Dutch Presence
in the Windsor-Detroit Border Region
by Joan Magee

Dundurn Local History Series: 2

Toronto and Charlottetown
Dundurn Press
1983

(In association with
The Netherlandic Press,
Windsor, Ontario)

Acknowledgements

The members of the Windsor Chapter of the Canadian Association for the Advancement of Netherlandic Studies wish to express their appreciation to the Department of the Secretary of State of Canada for the generous grant which allowed the preparation of the manuscript and publication of this book. The manuscript was originally prepared under the title "The Dutch Among Us — Two Hundred Years of Dutch Presence in Essex County"; the present title was chosen as being more indicative of the area studied.

For their encouragement and support, the author wishes to thank Ken Alexander, District Manager of the London Field Office of the Department of the Secretary of State of Canada, together with Yok Leng Chang and Eric Lugtigheid, Multiculturalism Directorate, Department of the Secretary of State of Canada; Albert Mate, University Librarian of the University of Windsor; Dhr. D.L. van den Berg and the librarians of the Emigration Service of the Government of the Netherlands in The Hague; Joan Reid, who typed the manuscript with her usual efficiency; R. Alan Douglas, for reading the manuscript in its earliest form and making helpful suggestions; Sylvia Thijs and Jenny Burridge for their tireless work as research assistants; and the members of the Dutch community of Windsor for their inspiration and support.

The publisher wishes to acknowledge the ongoing generous financial support of the Canada Council and the Ontario Arts Council.

J. Kirk Howard, Publisher

Copyright © Joan Magee

All rights reserved. No part of this publication may be reproduced, stored in a retrieval system, or transmitted in any form or by any means, electronic, mechanical, photocopying, recording or otherwise (except brief passages for purposes of review) without the prior permission of Dundurn Press Limited.

Editor: George Hancocks
Copyeditor: Blaine Beemer
Design: Ron and Ron Design Photography
Typesetting: Computype
Printed by: Les Editions Marquis, Montmagny, Quebec, Canada

Dundurn Press Limited
P.O. Box 245, Station F
Toronto, Canada
M4Y 2L5

Canadian Cataloguing in Publication Data

Magee, Joan.
    A Dutch Heritage

(Dundurn local history series; 2)
Bibliography: p.
Includes index.
ISBN 0-919670-66-0

I. Dutch — Ontario — Essex — History. I. Title.
II. Series.

FC3905.E77Z7 1983   971.3'310043931   C83-098528-X
F1059.E7M34

A Dutch Heritage
200 Years of Dutch Presence
in the Windsor-Detroit Border Region
by Joan Magee

Dundurn Local History Series: 2

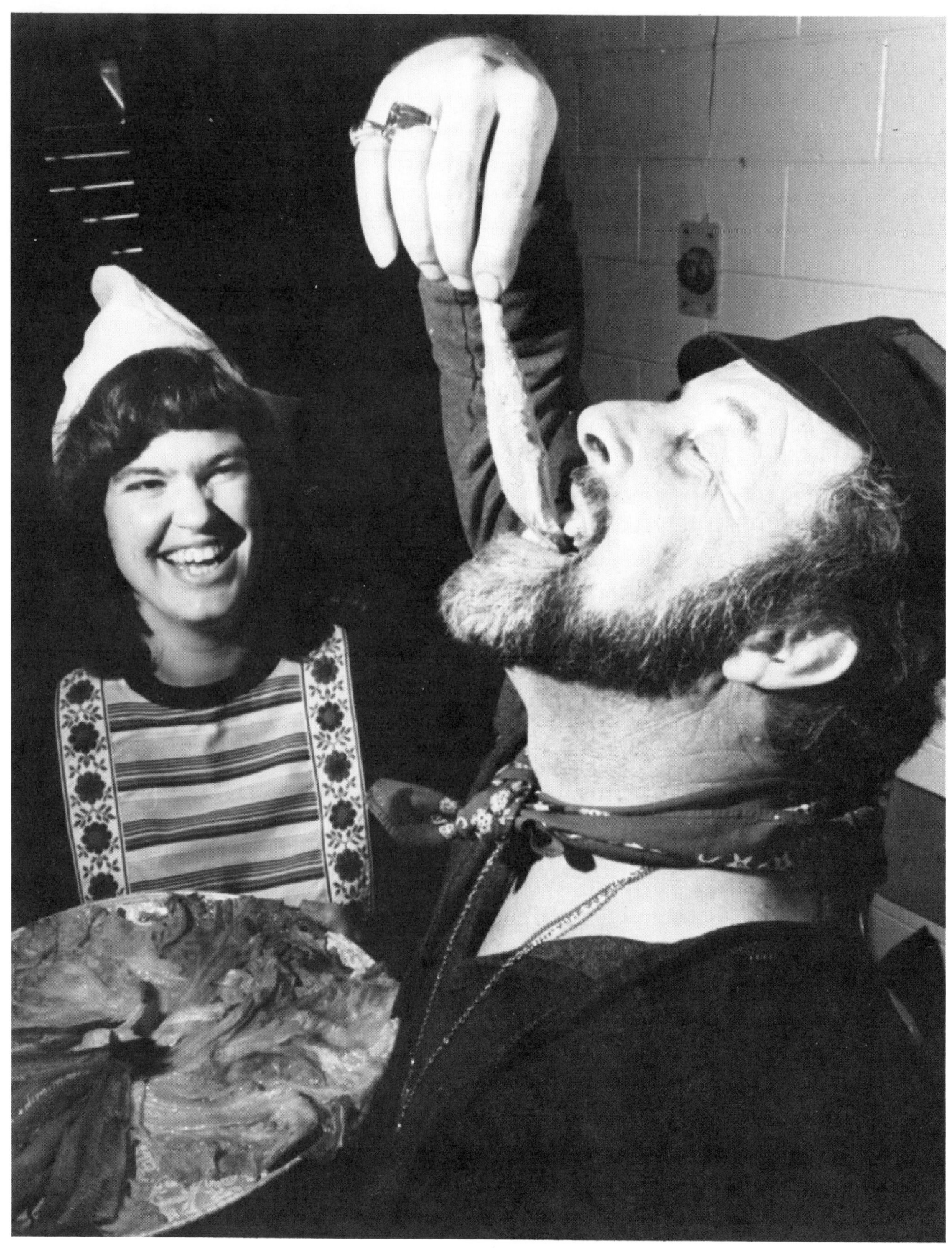

Henk De Laat demonstrates the traditional Dutch way of eating salted new herring to Margie Hopkins. *One of the most popular booths at the Old Dutch Village Market is the one where Henk De Laat sells smoked herring, mackerel, and* maatjes *(young) herring.*

Contents

Foreword	8
Preface	9
1. New Netherland: A Dutch Colony in America	11
2. Beginnings	15
3. The Pennsylvania Dutch	27
4. Dutch Immigrants for Michigan	31
5. Captain Henry Van Allen and Peter Frederick Verhoeff	33
6. Murder in the Mill	39
7. Descendants of the Loyalists	43
8. Sir William Cornelius Van Horne	47
9. Dutch Immigration to Canada 1892-1913	49
10. Immigration Between the Wars, 1919-1939	55
11. Post-War Immigration 1946-1960	61
12. Development of a Dutch Community	67
13. Growth of a Dutch Community: the Churches	77
14. Dutch Social Clubs	85
15. The Dutch in Essex County in the 1980s: A Survey	93
16. It Wasn't Easy	109
Appendix 1: The Windsor Chapter of CAANS	111
Appendix 2: Population of Canada Reporting Netherlandic Origin, 1871-1981	121
Appendix 3: Population of Tri-County Area Reporting Ethnic or Racial Origin as Netherlands, 1921-1971	121
Notes	122
Selected Bibliography	124
Photography Index and Credits	125
Index	126

Foreword

It will be obvious to anyone familiar with Essex County's topography that those who consider only its heights of land are missing a great deal. Similarly, those who see only "the Indians" — whatever that vague term means — succeeded by the French and then the British, do themselves a great disservice by overlooking the depth and the variety of the county's ethnic landscape.

It is true that the groups just mentioned have, by reason of the historical process, been largely responsible for the character of life in the Essex Peninsula. Others, however, from the Albanians to the Zimbabweans, have contributed important variations. Joan Magee has called attention to the Dutch presence in the region, a presence all the more easily overlooked because of the long-established confusion of the Dutch with the larger German (*Deutsch*) element in the population. For this important beginning to a better appreciation of the complexity of our heritage, we are indebted to her.

R. Alan Douglas
Curator,
Hiram Walker Historical Museum
Windsor, Ontario

December 1982

Preface

The land along the south and east shores of the Detroit River in what is now Essex County is of great historical interest, for it is the oldest continuously settled area in the Province of Ontario. It was first populated according to a regular plan of settlement by the French 1749-1751. As the years passed, the first French farmers were joined by those Detroit citizens who wished to remain under the British flag, and later by immigrants of many nationalities from other parts of Canada, the United States, and overseas. It was only some 20 years after the first farms were laid out that the first settlers of Dutch origin arrived. From this time on, there has been a steady stream of Dutch immigrants; a mere trickle at times, but always a noticeable element in the development of the population through the past 200 years.

In this book, I shall attempt to trace the Dutch presence in Essex County during the past two centuries. Included will be not only those settlers who came directly from the Netherlands, but also those who arrived by other routes, such as the United Empire Loyalists from New York, some of the Pennsylvania Dutch, and certain Mennonites from Russia. They share a common heritage, for at one point in their family history their ancestors left the Netherlands and made their way, directly or indirectly, towards a home in Essex County.

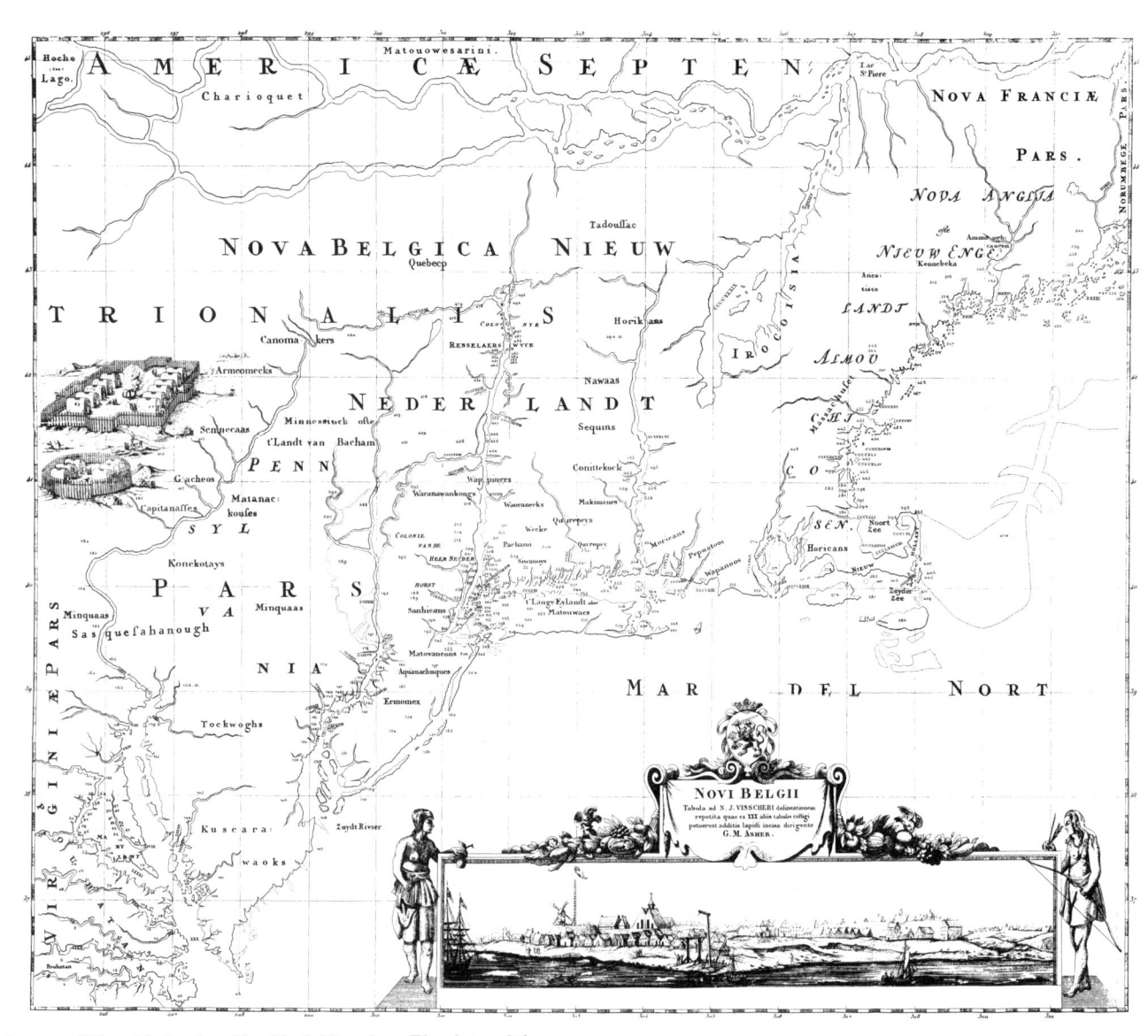

A map of New Netherland by N. J. Visscher. The date of the map is about 1650 to 1656.

1

New Netherland:
A Dutch Colony In America

In 1609 the English explorer Henry Hudson was placed in command of a Dutch three-masted ship, and given the task of finding a new route to the Far East. While trying to do so, he discovered the river which is now named after him. His reports to the Dutch authorities about the quality and great number of beaver skins which the Indians seemed prepared to trade soon led to the establishment of small Dutch trading posts along the Hudson River Valley. Eventually the Dutch laid claim to a huge area between the Delaware and Connecticut rivers, and agents of the West Indian Trading Company, which had been carrying on a profitable trade in West Africa, Brazil, and the West Indies, set up permanent trading posts. Eventually the company received the exclusive trading rights to the area, which was now officially named New Netherland.[1]

Few Dutch were willing to settle in the new colony. Economic conditions were so good in the Netherlands that this period has become known as the "Golden Age". Word had spread about the crowded ships and the number who died from disease. Persons of other nationalities who wished to emigrate for religious reasons, such as the English Puritans, had a much stronger incentive than did the Dutch, since at this time the Netherlands was itself a haven for the persecuted of Europe. The population of the English colonies grew at a much faster rate, so that by 1664 the English in America outnumbered the Dutch by ten to one. That year, when New Netherland was captured by the English, it had a total population of 8,000 to 10,000. Only two-thirds of this number were Dutch, and many of these had been born in America. As we shall see, one of the chief reasons that the colony fell to the British was a lack of colonists.

A hundred years later, the Dutch farmers of New Netherland had scattered throughout the British colonies of the eastern seaboard, although the greatest number were to be found in the areas of former Dutch domination — the states of New York and New Jersey. In the later colonial period, only a few emigrants from the Netherlands came to America, most of them settling in New York like their predecessors. This trickle of Dutch immigration continued until the early days of the American Republic. After the Napoleonic Wars, there was a decided increase followed by a great upsurge between 1840 and 1860. In that period more than 20,000 Dutch settlers arrived in the United States, and during the rest of the century great numbers of Dutch immigrants continued to pour into the country.

Many of these later immigrants had left the Netherlands because they could not practise their religion as they pleased. Now in the Netherlands was great poverty and unrest, and by 1850 more than one-quarter of the Dutch population were unemployed. There was devastating flooding of the low-lying reclaimed lands, and many had to abandon their homes. The potato blight struck, bringing famine and suffering. All these reasons provided an impetus to the Dutch to emigrate to America in large numbers throughout the nineteenth century.

The Dutch chose the United States as their preferred immigration land, in particular settling in Michigan, Iowa, and Wisconsin, where they founded large colonies. Few went to British North America which at that time was attracting large numbers of English, Irish, and Scottish settlers.

Migration to the area now known as Essex County reflected these trends. Dutch immigrants of the period 1770-1891 came almost exclusively by way of the eastern states where the Dutch had settled in the seventeenth century, or via the midwest, in particular from Michigan. The number of such immigrants was small, and they must be thought of as individual settlers. However, as will be seen, from the earliest days of pioneer settlement the Dutch have been present continuously in the border area.

View of Amsterdam from the formerly open *IJ*, detail of an engraving by G. Temini, mid-17th century. *From here, the ships of the Dutch West Indian Company left for New Netherland.*

The *Grote Markt*, the market place of Haarlem in 1627 or 1628. *This scene would have been familiar to Jean de Peyster who was born in Haarlem and emigrated to New Netherland around 1645. This etching, made by Jan van de Velde after a painting by P. Saenredam, was used as an illustration in the seventeenth-century book Beschrijvinge by S. Ampzing. The verse may be freely translated as follows:*

Here you see the palace that King William made
his court
And royal dwelling place. Both earlier and later on
This court was in Haarlem; it was the ducal palace,
to our honour and glory.

Now the city hall is here, there, on the side of the
street,
With the council busy creating good laws,
Where right is pronounced whenever there is dis-
agreement,
And where those who go against the laws are punished.

How can a land exist where good customs
And laws are trodden down?
Along with the soul, the body is the support of life;
And so is righteousness the lifeline of the land.

[author's translation]

This oil painting of Col. Arent Schuyler De Peyster is now in
the collection of the King's Museum of Liverpool, England.

2

Beginnings

By the eighteenth century the tide of settlement pressed ever westward, and with it came pioneers of Dutch[1] ancestry — descendants of Netherlanders who had already settled in the New World.

The twin forces of trade and revolution brought Col. Arent Schuyler De Peyster to what is now Essex County, and he arrived in the Detroit River area in 1779 not to settle, but to serve as British commandant of Detroit, then an important outpost of British North America. He is probably the first major representative of the Dutch presence in the border region, and this American-born soldier of Dutch descent was to have a lasting influence on the settlement in the few short years he served there.

De Peyster was raised in New York City when some still lived who could remember it as New Amsterdam, capital of the Dutch colony of New Netherland. Born 27 June 1736, he was the son of Pierre Guillaume De Peyster (Peter De Peyster) and Cornelia Schuyler, daughter of Arent Schuyler and his second wife, Swantje Dyckhuyse.

The De Peysters (whose name means "the countryman") were descendants of an old Flemish family from the Ghent area, and were well connected in New Amsterdam. They had connections by marriage to many *patroon*[2] families, including the Schuyler family, founded by Philip Pietersen Schuyler of Amsterdam, of which Arent's mother was a member.

While there is no evidence that Arent made use of his mother tongue during his years of service in Detroit, he probably did so. He would certainly have found his knowledge of the language useful in dealing with the Moravians and their Indian converts, who spoke a form of Low German not unlike Dutch, and with Dutch-speaking settlers among Loyalist refugees from the states of New York, New Jersey, and Pennsylvania. However, English was his main language throughout his life, though he could also speak and write French with great fluency, an important ability in Detroit with its French origins.

Following his father's example, De Peyster chose a military career, and in 1755 was commissioned third lieutenant in the Independent Company of Grenadiers of the City of New York. Later he served with the Eighth Regiment of Foot (King's Liverpool Regiment), and was stationed in Ireland and Germany before returning to North America in 1768.

With the threat of revolution hanging over the

Map of the Netherlands.

English colonies, his regiment was sent to garrison the strategic forts of Niagara, Detroit, and Michilimackinac. For the five years 1774 to 1779, De Peyster, now a Captain, was in command of the troops at Michilimackinac[3], an important fur trading post, and there he developed a respect for Indians which was to last the rest of his life. His role at the fort was to keep the goodwill of his Indian allies, strengthen the fort, and increase British prestige. He was an ideal choice for the position. A loyal colonial, he understood the needs and problems of the Indians, traders, and settlers, and had the advantage of an upbringing in a prominent military family with English sympathies.

In 1779, with the American Revolution at its height, he was promoted major, made commandant of Detroit, and dispatched by boat from Michilimackinac with orders to create a modern British fort to replace the old French fortifications.[4] The new fort, known as Fort Lernoult, eventually became Fort Shelby when the Americans took over the settlement.

De Peyster's friendship with the Indians and his real concern about their welfare led to one other important development in local history which was to have implications for later Dutch settlers. As commandant of Detroit, he ordered a group of Moravians to leave their settlement near Pittsburgh and move to Detroit.

The Moravian missionaries and their orderly, peaceful colony of Delaware Indians had been caught up in the Revolutionary War through an unfortunate set of circumstances. Since they lived in a district made dangerous by roving bands of warlike Indians, as well as white settlers bent on revenge for Indian raids, they had issued a note of warning to the Americans, solely as a benevolent act.

This action, however, had managed to anger the British, who tried to break up the missions and separate the missionaries from their converts. Thus orders came from De Peyster that the missionaries should appear in Detroit to answer to charges of "meddling with Public Matters".[5] Virtual prisoners, the Moravian group, led by David Zeisberger, travelled to judgement.

De Peyster questioned them closely regarding the reasons for their behaviour, then decided they had been acting in charity, and publicly declared them free to return to their camping grounds in Sandusky. He also supplied them with clothes for themselves and their families, gave them fresh horses (for theirs had been stolen in Detroit), supplies and, most important of all, a passport permitting them to "perform the functions of [their] office among the Christian Indians without molestation".[6]

De Peyster's command of Detroit coincided with a period of great upheaval on the frontiers, and by 1784, when his tour of duty was over, Canada had received a massive influx of United Empire Loyalists — a group that also included many of Dutch ancestry. One branch of the Dolsen family of New York State, for instance, had taken up residence in the fort of Detroit as early as the 1760s. Although not much is known of them, a son, Matthew Dolsen, was born there about 1770, nearly a decade before De Peyster's arrival.

This Matthew Dolsen (c1770-c1813), however, must be distinguished from the better known and somewhat older Matthew Dolsen (d.1813) who fought with Butler's Rangers as a Loyalist and opened a tavern and store in Detroit in 1781.[7] Not only are the two names identical; they lived in the same area at about the same time, both leaving Detroit near the end of the eighteenth century to settle along the banks of the Thames. Both men, however, did represent two different branches of the Dutch Dolsen family, and both originated in New York State where the family had settled after its arrival from the Netherlands in the seventeenth century.

The Dolsen name has changed many times: germanized from van Dolsen and van Dalsen to Van Dolzen; anglicized to Dalston, Dolsen, and finally Dolsen; and, in fact, is also spelled several other ways by various members of this large and widespread pioneer family.

The original name was van Dalfsen, and the family was of Dutch, not German origin.[8] The founding ancestor of the van Dalfsen family in America was Jan Gerritsen van Dalfsen or "Dalsen", from the village of Dalfsen or the surrounding area, in the Province of Overijssel in the eastern part of the Netherlands.

He arrived in New Amsterdam about the middle of the seventeenth century and settled, probably as a tenant, on one of the great patroonships or patents in the Hudson River Valley. A descendant, Isaac Dolsen, founded one of the original pioneer families of Wyoming Township in Northumberland County and became a successful landowner. He was a strong supporter of the Loyalist cause, and during the American Revolution, because of his sympathies, was forced to abandon the family farm in the Manor of Sunbury (which was later confiscated) and escape with his family to Niagara in 1778.

Isaac's son Matthew, who was farming independently, also suffered greatly because of his support of the Loyalist cause:

> ... he was harassed and imprisoned in Northumberland Jail on account of his loyalty to the British Government, and was obliged to leave his farm, and lost his crop and all his cattle and stock as the rebels threatened his life. He fled to York to join General Clinton, and was taken and imprisoned and one of his brothers was killed by his side.... He made his escape after being long confined, and came in to Niagara, and since to this place [Detroit].[9]

In the same group of Loyalist refugees as the Dolsens were the Fields, close neighbours in Pennsylvania and related by marriage. In Niagara, Isaac and Matthew Dolsen and two of the three Field sons, Daniel and Nathan, joined Butler's Rangers, a Loyalist force under the command of Lieutenant Colonel John Butler. For three years they fought the rebels, in 1778 in their native Wyoming Valley, later in other territory.

Then, in 1781, during De Peyster's regime, Matthew Dolsen arrived in Detroit, perhaps as a soldier with Butler's Rangers, for the regiment was stationed in Detroit for some time. It is certain he was there as early as May 1781, for he purchased a lot in the fort from Gregor McGregor and began to work as a trader and merchant. Eventually, he kept an inn.

Meanwhile, Isaac Dolsen remained in Niagara with other members of his large family. He settled there when Butler's regiment was disbanded late in 1784, but was greatly disappointed in the arrangement made for Loyalist farmers, and was one of the chief petitioners in a formal complaint about the situation. Eventually he also moved to the Detroit River region, buying on 2 September 1784 a farm at Petite Côte on the east side of the Detroit River, for which he paid £500 to the French farmer, Theophile Lemay, who had developed it. Isaac thus became the first person of Dutch heritage to settle in the area now known as Essex County.

He was followed just a week later by his son-in-law, Daniel Field, who bought the adjoining lot. However, Field soon sold it to Matthew, who by then had a well-established inn and store in Detroit. Matthew did not live on his Petite Côte farm, but visited it from time to time. In 1793 he took visiting Quakers who were staying at his inn in Detroit over by boat to see his farm, where they ate cherries from Dolsen's trees.[10]

Isaac added at least one child to his large family while living at Petite Côte, for a descendant stated that his grandfather was born at "Sandwich" in 1785.[11] Soon, however, Isaac became a squatter in the Valley of the Lower Thames. As elsewhere in the province at the time, Dolsen like other settlers was technically a squatter on Indian land, both here and at Petite Côte. The problem was not resolved until 1790 when most of the land which is now Essex County was bought from the Indians with trade goods. A survey made by Patrick McNiff in 1790 shows the Isaac Dolsen farm on the south side, in what would become Raleigh Township. This is the farm on which the Dolsens live to this day.[12]

By 1789 Matthew Dolsen had also established himself on the Thames River in what is now Dover Township, across the river from his father, dividing his time between managing his Detroit inn (where his family lived only at times), farming at Petite Côte, and making frequent trips to his establishment and permanent home on the Thames. Not until 1792 did he receive an official grant on the Thames (for land which he had meantime improved), and began to receive provisions as a Loyalist. Yet he continued to live part of the year in Detroit, still being listed there in 1796 as a resident who wanted to remain under the British flag.

Although the Americans had won their independence in 1783, the British refused to abandon Detroit and other ports in the western region. This was an attempt to pressure them into compensating Loyalists such as the Dolsens for their property losses. As much as ten years after the end of the war, English fur traders and such Canadian settlers as Matthew Dolsen still continued to carry out profitable fur trading in what was technically American territory. When Detroit finally passed officially to the Americans in 1796, the town became American in fact as well as name, and Matthew moved permanently to his estate on the Thames, where his descendants remained until the farm was sold in 1915.

Interestingly enough, Matthew was closely associated with the same Moravian missionaries and their Indian converts helped by De Peyster. Although in 1781 De Peyster had provided the destitute Moravians with food from the King's store in Detroit, and had written to Moravians in England for donations, this had not been sufficient. Zeisberger turned to Matthew Dolsen for help. Although he knew the newly-arrived innkeeper was himself not in particularly good circumstances, Zeisberger asked for assistance with the words:

> There are, we know, many wealthier gentlemen in this place than you are, who could help us if they would, but perhaps they are not so worthy of doing it. We ask that favour of you.[13]

Dolsen agreed. Thus, it is not surprising that from the fall of 1791 to the spring of 1792, the two Dolsen children, Isaac and John, attended a short-lived mission school set up by the Moravians at a point near present-day Amherstburg. There, in 1791, the missionaries were allowed to settle on Colonel Alexander McKee's plantation of 2,000 acres and use Matthew Elliott's large house on his neighbouring land downriver, while the Indian converts camped on the grounds between. Soon a church was built and the settlement given a name: "Die Warte", or "The Watch Tower".

A number of records in David Zeisberger's diary show the young Dolsen children among those attending the school, taught by Brother Gottlob Sensemann.[14] John, 15, eldest of the two, was born about 1776 in Fishing Creek, Pennsylvania, and was only two when the family escaped to Niagara. Isaac, the second son, born in Detroit on 23 August 1786, was only five when he went to school at Die Warte.

On Tuesday, 12 April 1792, the Moravians assembled for the last time in their chapel at Die Warte, and the school was closed in preparation for a move to the Thames and a new settlement they named Fairfield. The two Dolsen boys returned to their home in Detroit and eventually to the Dolsen farm on the Thames, not far downriver from the Moravians.

The Matthew Dolsen Thames settlement continued to grow into an impressive estate. Soon it included a gristmill, distillery, tavern, and blacksmith's shop.

The castle known as "Huis Rechteren" in Dalfsen, Overijssel province, the Netherlands. *The view is taken from the dike just outside the village of Dalfsen. This dike and the view of the castle would have been familiar landmarks to the Dutch ancestors of the Dolsens (originally the "van Dalfsen" family). The defense tower of the castle dates from the fourteenth century.*

A typical farmhouse or *hoeve* of Dalfsen, in Overijssel province in the Netherlands. *Such houses are typical of this village, after which the Dolsen (or "van Dalfsen") family was named. Living quarters are in the front of the large farmhouse. The hearth is located in the livingroom-kitchen in a safe place to avoid fire, always a hazard when the roofing is of thatch. The farm animals are housed in the largest part of the* hoeve, *in the back of this building with its large and characteristic doorway.*

In 1789, Dolsen even built an 80-ton pine-timbered boat for the North West Company, to be used in the fur trade. He continued to enlarge his estate, retiring only a few years before his death in 1813. The plantation became known simply as "Dolsen's", and was the chief settlement in the area, although it waned in importance compared to the growing town of Chatham in the 1820s and 1830s.

Before leaving the Dolsen family, mention must be made of the "other Matthew Dolsen", who was born in Detroit about 1770 and died about 1813, shortly after the Battle of the Thames in which he took part. Nothing could more clearly illustrate the divisive effect of the American Revolution than the contrast between the "Loyal" and the "Rebel" Dolsens. The Rebel Dolsen settled on the Thames at about the same time as his namesake, raising a family of five together with his wife, Elizabeth Willits of Detroit, formerly of Pennsylvania.

When the war of 1812 broke out, he was pressed into the British Army and taken from the Thames to Sandwich. There he deserted and escaped to Detroit to join Hull's army. When General Hull surrendered Detroit, Dolsen scaled the pickets and fled to Chillicothe, Ohio. There, because of his knowledge of the Thames River area, he became an asset to the Americans when they invaded in 1813. He acted as a guide for the invaders, and was present at the Battle of Moraviantown, when the mission was burned to the ground. Meanwhile, Dolsen's wife and five young children, all under eight years of age, moved from the Thames to Detroit on 20 October 1813. There the family moved in with the Willits and this branch of the Dolsen family remained in Detroit where its members have been active in business circles for the past century.

Though Matthew and Isaac Dolsen were in the forefront of those U.E. Loyalists who arrived early in the Detroit border area, the close of the American Revolution in 1783 brought with it a surge of Loyalist immigrants who wished to settle under the British flag. They brought new life to an area which had remained an isolated French settlement during the 23 years of British occupation since 1760.

There were many Dutch among the refugees who crowded into Canada by the thousands in the mid-1780s, including ancestors of many of the citizens of Essex County. The major battles of the Revolution had been fought in areas heavily populated with Dutch settlers, and the war forced them to choose between Whig or Tory. While a few Dutch took the Whig side and joined the rebels, many more supported the King and served voluntarily in Loyalist regiments raised in 1776 and the following five years. In some cases, families were split in their loyalty, even in the most aristocratic houses. The De Peyster family, for instance, boasted two well-known military men: one a Whig and rebel, General Philip Schuyler, the other a Tory, Major (later Colonel) Arent Schuyler De Peyster. In New York State alone, out of a population of 180,000, there were some 90,000 Loyalists, of whom 35,000 opposed the Revolution and fled to Canada.

Some writers believe many Dutch were Loyalists because they were accustomed to the authority of the Dutch Reformed Church, and conservative in religion and politics. It is true that when the English captured New Netherland, they permitted the Dutch to continue the Dutch-language services of the Reformed Church. They also brought with them the Anglican Church, a state church of which the King was head, and loyalty to the sovereign was soon shared by the conservative Dutch.

Then too, the Dutch settlers had never been particularly satisfied with the government during the period when the West Indian Company merchants controlled the colony, and ruled it for commercial gain. Most Dutch felt they were better off under British rule, and remained loyal for this reason. Moreover, the great landowners, the *patroons*, tended to distrust rebel, democratic movements which could encourage tenants to demand better living and working conditions on their manorial estates.

Whatever their reasons, Loyalists of Dutch descent came from New York, New Jersey, and Pennsylvania, and tended to arrive in Canada along the border at Niagara and Kingston. A few came from Pennsylvania directly to Detroit. At first, the refugees were housed in temporary quarters, and there was great suffering. Many died, particularly the elderly, the weak, and the very young. Those who survived the first months were offered a wide choice of land on which to settle, and many of Dutch descent settled around Niagara, the Bay of Quinte and north shore of the St. Lawrence, Nova Scotia, New Brunswick or Quebec. Fewer of the descendants of these Loyalists have come to live in Essex County, although a notable exception is the Van Buskirk family from Shelburne, Nova Scotia.

Loyalist settlement at Detroit was deliberately kept to a minimum, perhaps because it was an isolated outpost, and vulnerable, or because the government was afraid Detroit might attract a large number of rebel sympathizers. Sir Frederick Haldimand was careful to choose who could settle there, and did not make many land grants in the area. By comparison with the settlements at Niagara and Quinte, grants made in what is now Essex County were few[15] nor were there many Loyalists of Dutch heritage in this small number. Still, there were some.

Among those who wanted to settle in Essex were soldiers who had belonged to Butler's Rangers, and who had seen service under Captain William Caldwell in Detroit during the war. Following disbandment at Niagara in 1784, Caldwell obtained a tract of land on the shore of Lake Erie, as close as possible to the mouth of the Detroit River, and named it the New Settlement, as distinct from the old settlements at L'Assomption and Petite Côte. Patrick McNiff of Detroit was appointed deputy-surveyor of the District of Hesse (the name given to a newly

DOLSEN'S.[1]

"Dolsen's", the pioneer farm on the Thames River about four kilometres below Chatham on the north bank of the Thames river, as sketched in 1860 by Benson J. Lossing. *The artist described the house as a hewn-log structure owned by Isaac Dolsen, then over 80 years old and living in Chatham. Dolsen and his brother John were said to be of Dutch descent and natives of the Mohawk Valley. They were sons of Matthew Dolsen, the Loyalist and trader. Isaac inherited the property after his father's death, and was resident there during the bitter fighting of the War of 1812.*

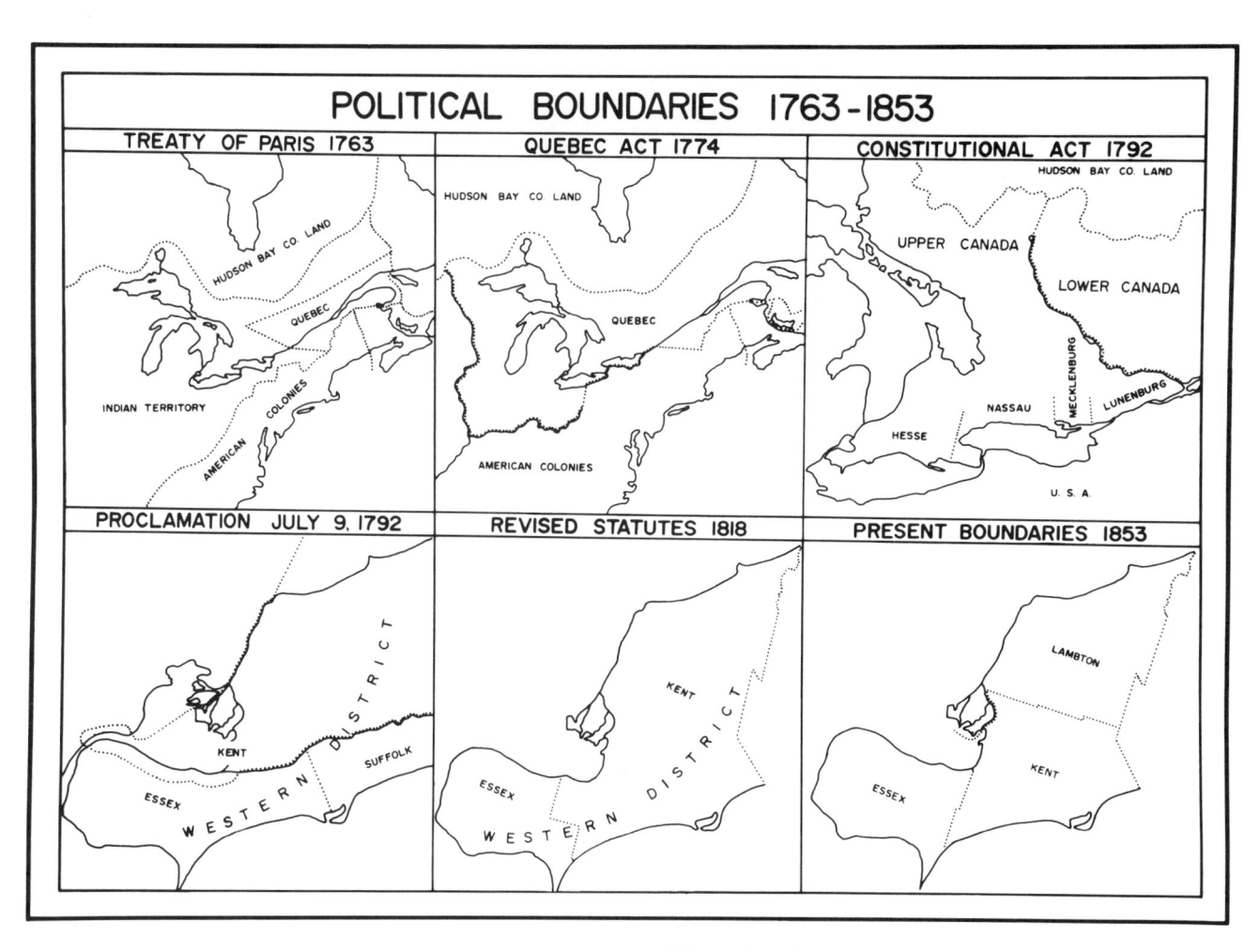

This series of maps show the frequent changes in political boundaries made from 1763 to 1853; *the boundaries of Essex County set up in that final year are the ones still in use today.*

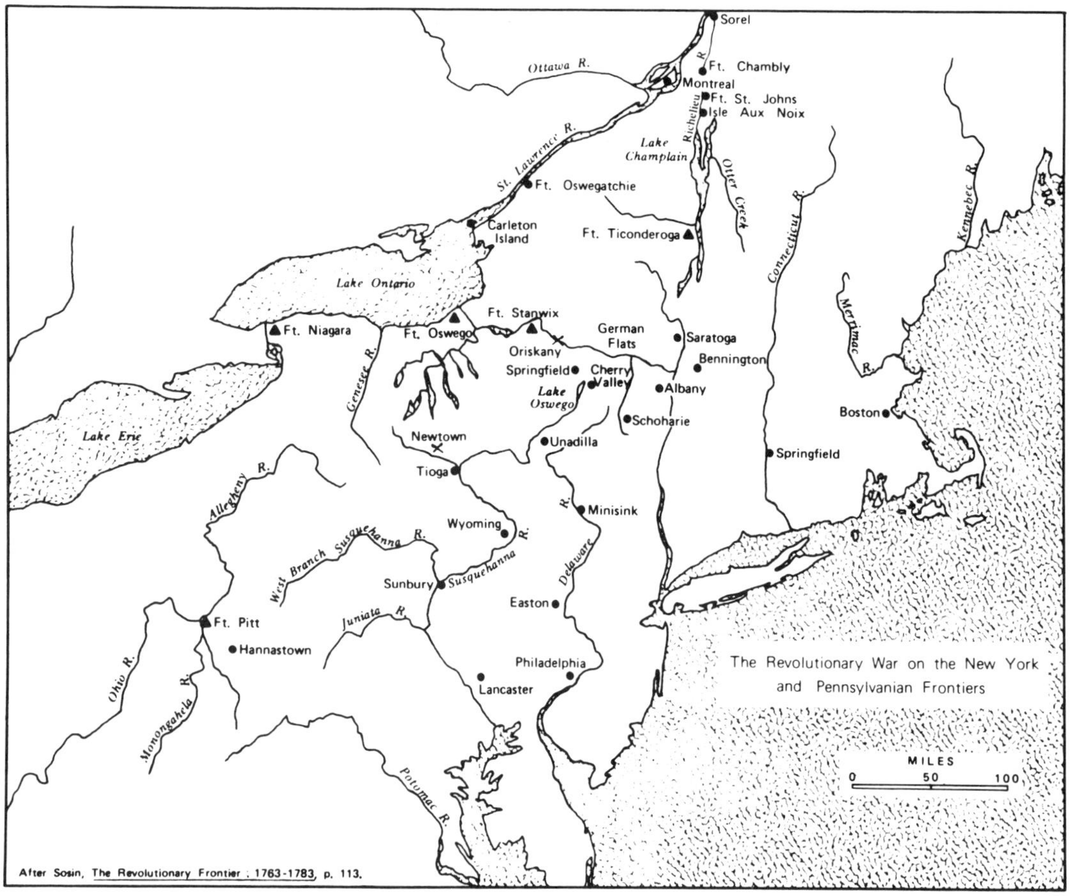

After Sosin, The Revolutionary Frontier : 1763-1783, p. 113.

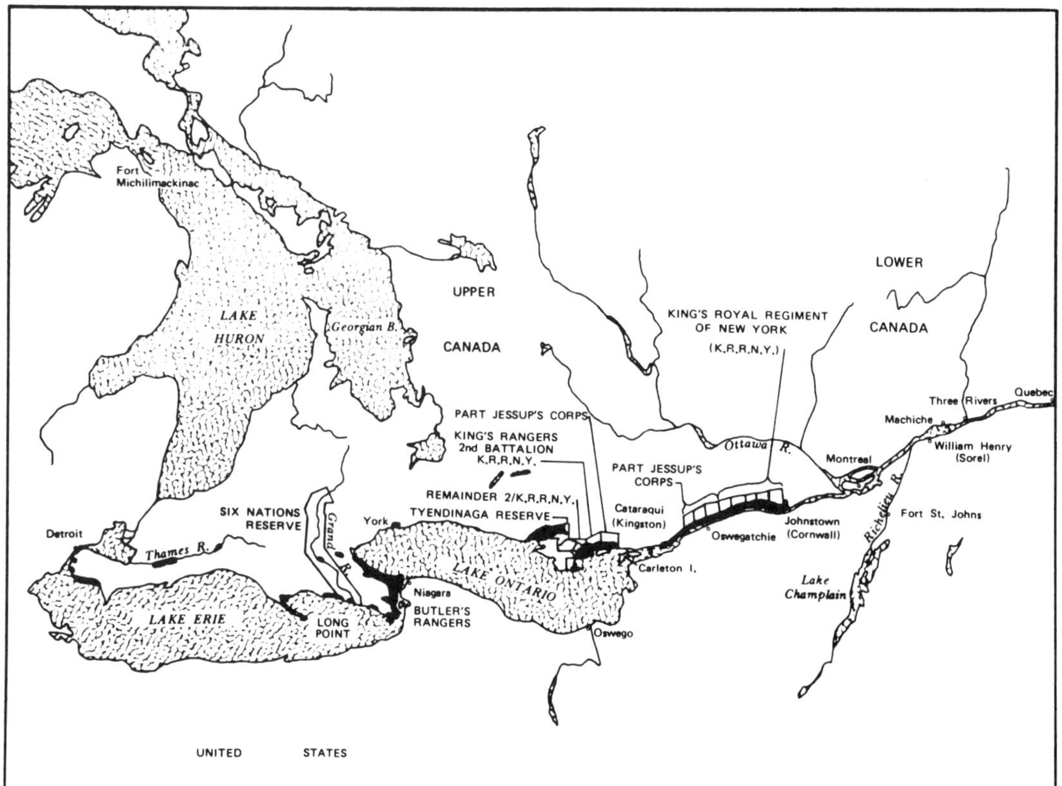

After Kerr, A Historical Atlas of Canada, p. 36.

created area which included what is now Essex County) and laid out 97 lots "in the best manner that could then be done by the best surveyor they then could provide".[16]

The location, name and occupations of these settlers were provided for General Haldimand on lists still in existence. Some Dutch names appear among the families listed as owning lots close to what is now the town of Colchester, among them the name of Vancamp, showing that a father and son of this name had fought together in the Royal Regiment of New York, and had been assigned town lots. The Christian names of the Vancamps are not available, and it is unfortunately not possible to trace them further. The only other reference to them is found in the Haldimand Papers at the Public Archives of Canada where a letter from General Haldimand to Brigadier General H. Watson Powell, written on 31 May 1782, says:

> And if Colo. Proctor's Intelligence thro' Vancamp by the son is to have any credit the Enemy's designs against the Upper Country are eventualy [sic], depending entirely upon the evacuation of Charlestown.[17]

From this, it would appear the Vancamps were serving as scouts and intelligence officers.

While they were both issued lots, it is apparent they either did not claim them, or left soon after they did so, discouraged with conditions in the settlement. The location did not offer as attractive a situation as many elsewhere, including those along the banks of the Thames River. Many Lake Erie settlers also found their lots were too wet to produce crops. As Loyalists, they had been promised provisions and tools, but these failed to arrive. By 1794, when a survey of the area was taken by Patrick McNiff, only a few of the original settlers were still on their lots. The rest, including the Vancamps, had gone elsewhere.

In that same year, a report of the Land Committee pressed for immediate relief for "certain discharged Rangers, Loyalists and others now residing at, and near Detroit".[18] The report quotes minutes of the Land Board of Hesse which paint a sorry picture of settlers taking up land by drawing lots, then being unable to improve their properties because of lack of provisions and tools. To add insult to injury, many lost those unimproved lots, which were later handed out by draw to others. Those who persevered found lots on the Thames (River la Franche[19]), and still felt they were entitled to the promised provisions and tools, as well as title to their now-improved lots. The committee agreed with the Land Board and specified that any discharged Ranger or Loyalist who could prove to the board their entitlement to land, and who did not take up land elsewhere "should now be located and provisioned ... and ... that they be issued ... monthly, and upon proof they were actually improving their Lands".

While the Vancamps had left the area in discouragement and could not take advantage of this new offer, the Dolsens were among those who did. Having settled on the Thames River, made their claims and offered proof of the improvement of their lands, they eventually started to receive provisions and land grants that put them in an advantageous position as Loyalist settlers.

There were other members of the Vancamp, or "Van Camp" family who did settle permanently in Ontario, sons of Peter Van Camp, a Loyalist who died in Montreal in 1783. The two Van Camp sons, Jacob and John, both of whom settled in Matilda, Dundas County, were the ancestors of many Van Camps in Ontario, including some who later came to live in Essex. However, the Van Camp family connected with Stokely-Van Camp, the canning factory active for many years in the town of Essex, is not the Ontario family of that name, but rather an American branch from the midwestern United States. The American Van Camps, like the Canadians of that name, are, however, descended from three settlers who came to New Netherland about 1650 from Kampen on the Zuiderzee.

Other Dutch among the earliest settlers of the so-called "New Settlement" included Julious [Julius?] and Frederick Rapely, of the Rapelje family of New York State. Although it remains unclear which branch of the family they came from, the Dutch-speaking Rapeljes were descendants of Antonie Jansen de Rapelje, brother of George, leader of the Walloon families which settled at the "Wallabout" on Long Island. After some years had passed and surnames were chosen, George adopted "Jansen" ("John's son") as his surname. Eventually, under English rule, the name of this branch of the family became Johnston. The descendants of Antonie de Rapelje dropped the "Jansen de" from the name and became the Rapely, Rapelje, and Rapelye families.[20]

The 1794 McNiff survey, however, revealed the Rapely family was no longer living on its "New Settlement" lands, and eventually the Land Board of Hesse reassigned them. It was not until the present generation that members of the Rapelje family moved again to Essex County.

By 1790, the settlement on the Lake Erie waterfront was enlarged and named the "Two Connected Townships in the New Settlement, Lake Erie". Within two or three years, the waterfront settlement was well established, making it the oldest community in Essex County other than the original French settlement. The county was beginning to fill up.

Button Wood Tree, painted circa 1840 by Lt. Philip John Bainbrigge (1817-1881). *The original watercolour over pencil is one of the sketches in a book carried by Lt. Bainbrigge on his travels throughout the Western District. In his sketchbook the artist painted scenes of pioneer life in the bush, the military operations he observed, and daily life in such communities as Chatham and Amherstburg. A close observation of this sketch of a pioneer clearing his land helps one appreciate the difficulties faced by these early settlers in southwestern Ontario, where much of the land remained covered with dense forest (this buttonwood tree measured 18 feet in girth) until the middle of the nineteenth century.*

3

The Pennsylvania Dutch

Among the first settlers of the Two Connected Townships along Lake Erie were Hessians[1] who had fought for the British against the American rebels, and Pennsylvania Dutch, the Mennonite pacifists who were considered pro-British because they had refused to bear arms. Among them were families with the surnames Kratz, Weigele, Eiler, and Fuchs (later anglicized to Scratch, Wigle, Iler, and Fox). These pioneers of Gosfield were of German background with possibly a strong admixture of Dutch, for they reported themselves repeatedly as being of Dutch origin in the official censuses of 1861, 1871, and 1881. In fact, according to these documents, Gosfield had a large Dutch population — apparent once the census figures were separated into "Dutch" and "German" in 1871 and 1881 rather than simply grouped together under "German and Dutch" as they had been in 1851 and 1861. In 1871, Gosfield was recorded as having 287 Dutch and 533 Germans, and in 1881, 509 Dutch and 364 Germans.[2] In 1891, ethnic origin or "nationality" was not asked.

Gosfield's Mennonites were often thought to be Dutch by their English-speaking neighbours because of confusion between the words "Dutch" and the German word for themselves, "Deutsch". Most belonged to a German-speaking group of settlers from New Jersey and Pennsylvania, with a strong element of Dutch in their seventeenth and early eighteenth century background.

Although a few Pennsylvania Dutch settled in Essex County in the 1780s and 1790s, it was between 1800 and 1837 that the first large-scale immigration took place. The main settlements were in Waterloo County, but some made their way to Essex.

Besides those who belong to pioneer families of Essex County itself, many residents of today can trace their ancestry to early settlers of the Waterloo area and neighbouring districts. The children of these Pennsylvania Dutch settlers were among those who claimed farms in the central part of the county, the last to be cleared before most of the best arable land was taken (about 1860) and large-scale immigration came to a temporary halt.

Clearing the land was heavy work, and settlers had to cut through one of the thickest forest walls in North America in order to begin cultivation. In 1824, William McCormick, a United Empire Loyalist who acted as an interpreter and trader with the Indians of this area, and eventually acquired Pelee Island and other lands in the County of Essex, wrote:

> Good Lands in a wild State may be bought at from twenty to forty Shillings per Acre according to their Situations — Lands of inferior qualities may be purchased much cheaper — Government will give to a poor Man not able to pay fees (being a British Subject) fifty Acres, subject to settling Duties which are to build a log-house, clear the road in front of his lot and clear for Cultivation five acres of Land.[3]
>
> The Man who has not got Money to purchase improved Lands can draw from the Government or purchase from Individuals if he thinks proper. Such Men should get on their Lands as soon as possible, raise a small Log-House to put his family in which he can do all within himself with about Ten or 12 days labour — His next care sh'd be to provide himself with a few Months provisions, a Cow, a Sow and a few Sheep, set his wife to spinning and himself to clear a piece of Land to put in a Crop as soon as possible — If he has no Neighbours to show him how to do his work, he should imatate [sic] the most industrious natives of the Country — If he has none such near him he should hire himself to one for a short time that will set him to work with People who are clearing Land that he may get into the Method of Clearing, at least so far as to use the Chopping Axe expertly.[4]

Along with the Pennsylvania Dutch came newcomers from Europe, as immigration was again made possible after the Napoleonic Wars. Most were from Great Britain, although some were from Germany and other European countries. By 1820 these newcomers began to arrive in considerable numbers, some making their way to Essex County:

> ... slow at first, the movement gained force in the 1820s and reached its height during the 1830s. After a brief check, it continued to grow during the 1840s, slackening gradually after 1855.[5]

The Scotch Settlement of the 1830s along the shore of Lake St. Clair, and much of the early English and Irish settlement of the county, date from this 35-year period. Few if any immigrants came directly from the Netherlands. One family came to Windsor via England, where some of their children had been born. In Canada they changed their name from Visscher to Fisher. But with this one exception, all the families of Dutch heritage came from other parts of Canada or the United States, and this remained the pattern throughout the entire nineteenth century.

While only scanty and undependable figures exist for emigration from the Netherlands during the early years of the nineteenth century, few Dutch left at this time. Most who did leave went to the Dutch East Indies, South Africa, or other parts of the world where the Dutch were a strong mercantile force. However, in the 1840s, large numbers of Dutch Seceders began to emigrate to the new Dutch colonies in Iowa and Western Michigan. While a few travelled through Canada, they moved on to join relatives and friends in the United States. The following letter, written by the Canadian emigration agent in Antwerp, Richard Berns, shows that Windsor in 1880 attracted immigrants who intended to make only a temporary stay in Canada:

> Anvers (Antwerp), 2nd June 1880
>
> The Honorable
> The Commissioner of Immigration
> Toronto
>
> Sir,
>
> ... "The Emigrants I have forwarded to Windsor [Ontario] declared me and signed that they would go and rejoin the parents and friends who were gone to Canada in the beginning of this year and settled in the Province of Ontario. I do not suppose that their intention was to go via Windsor to the United States, the much less as they could name me the persons who previously emigrated to Windsor, and that they could go cheaper via New York to any point in the United States. ... What regards the fact that Windsor lies on the frontier of the United States, that is not a reason which would prevent Immigrants of establishing themselves at Windsor and so remain in the Province of Ontario.
>
> I have the honour to be,
>
> Sir;
> Your obedient Servant,
> (Signed) Richard Berns[6]

View of Detroit from the Great Western Terminus in Windsor, circa 1860. *This watercolour painting by an unknown artist shows the terminus of the first railway to serve Windsor, the Great Western Railway. On 17 January 1854, the first passenger train to come through to Windsor from Niagara Falls arrived at this terminus. This memorable event caused great excitement in Windsor and marked the beginning of a new era in the development of the town. It rapidly grew in size as immigrants passed through on their way to the midwestern United States, or settled in the border area. Soon Windsor became a busy commercial centre, establishing itself as the largest community in the county of Essex.*

This copper engraving made in 1634 shows the cathedral city of Utrecht with its many windmills and impressive churches. *The van Allen family came to America from this ancient Dutch city, two of the brothers settling in New Amsterdam (now New York City) during the mid-1600s. The nave of the great cathedral, or Dom, was destroyed by a great storm in 1674, and never rebuilt.*

4

Dutch Immigrants For Michigan

The hamlet of Windsor changed little in the 1830s and 1840s, its population growing from only 200 in 1835 to about 750 on the eve of its incorporation as a village in 1854.

In 1837 the Irish author Anna Brownell Jameson compared Detroit and Windsor:

"... I have passed some hours straying or driving about on the British Shore.

"I hardly know how to convey to you an idea of the difference between the two shores; it will appear to you as incredible as it is to me incomprehensible. Our shore is said to be the most fertile, and has been the longest settled; but ... to behold on one side a city, with its towers and spires and animated population, with villas and handsome houses stretching along the shore, and a hundred vessels or more, gigantic steamers, brigs, schooners, crowding the port, loading and unloading; all the bustle, in short, of prosperity and commerce; — and, on the other side, a little straggling hamlet, one schooner, one little wretched steam-boat, some windmills, a catholic chapel or two, a supine ignorant peasantry, all the symptoms of apathy, indolence, mistrust, hopelessness! — can I, can any one, help wondering at the difference, and asking whence it arises?"[1]

Anna Jameson was wrong about the Canadian side being settled earlier than the American side, but she was quite accurate about the quietness of Windsor. This settlement was not to develop rapidly until arrival there of the Great Western Railway in 1854.

At the time of her visit there was already a steady stream of immigrants making their way through Canada to the Ferry, and across the Detroit River to Michigan, bound for the American midwest. Among them were few if any Dutch homesteaders — yet a decade later a large proportion of the America-bound immigrants were of Dutch origin. What had happened to cause this dramatic change?

One of the most important factors was the widespread poverty in the Netherlands. The industrial revolution came late to that country, and its citizens paid dearly for it. There were heavy taxes on such essentials as peat, coal, pork, mutton, and the grinding of grain. The poor could not afford to pay, nor could they avoid these taxes. Child labour was common; working conditions were appalling, with little reward for long hours of labour. When both a cholera epidemic and a potato blight struck in the 1840s, many Netherlanders turned to thoughts of emigration.

There were also religious reasons for the exodus. Except for about 1,000 Roman Catholics who left, most emigrants were Seceders. By 1856 there were at least 10,000 of these Seceders in the United States, settled chiefly in Michigan, Iowa, Illinois, and Wisconsin. In their native country they had not been allowed to set up their own "Christian Schools", nor to worship freely. They were required to accept the more liberal theology of the Reformed Church, the state church of the Netherlands — one to which they no longer wished to belong. They much preferred their Seceder churches based on orthodox Protestant principles.

Most Seceders came as families; even as entire congregations led by their own ministers. Among the latter were the followers of Rev. A.C. van Raalte, who in 1847 founded a colony in the uncleared wilderness of Western Michigan. From Wanneperveen in Overijssel province, van Raalte had come under the influence of Rev. Peter Scholte of Utrecht while still a theology student. Both men established their colonies in the spring of 1847, Rev. Scholte leading his flock to the more easily cleared land of Iowa. Van Raalte, travelling ahead, arrived in Detroit via the *Great Western* on the ship's last voyage of the 1846 season. Van Raalte was well received in Detroit by a Dutch-American attorney, Theodore Romeyn, and soon made many friends. During the winter of 1846-1847, he made plans for the colony and completed the necessary business and legal arrangements.

He was barely in time. By December 1846, Dutch immigrants, many coming by way of Windsor, began arriving by the hundreds. Most were penniless, with little or no knowledge of English.

Among the first settlers of the colony in Holland, Michigan, were ancestors of a large present-day Essex County family, the Huschilts of LaSalle.[2] Through the maternal side of the family, the Huschilts are descendants of Cornelis van Malsen, the first teacher and one of the first settlers of Zeeland, Michigan. He was a student of theology in Arnhem in 1846 when he was offered the position of teacher by a group of Zeelanders who were planning to go to America and wished to be assured of Christian instruction from the beginning of their life in the new country. On a promise of 100 guilders towards his expenses if he would agree to accompany the group, van Malsen accepted, and with his sister Cornelia and her fiance travelled with the Zeelanders to the United States. At first it was uncertain whether the group would join the Scholte colony in Iowa or van Raalte's Michigan settlement. The decision was left to the leader of the first ship to reach New York. Rev. Scholte, by coincidence, was in New York at the time and persuaded the group to set out for Iowa. Dissention arose at Buffalo, however, and the immigrants eventually chose Michigan. They arrived there on 27 June 1847.

Today, the Huschilts of LaSalle have the unusual opportunity to read letters their ancestor wrote from the Michigan colony back home to his father, a teacher in Zwijndrecht. These letters, telling of his trip to America and his experiences in the Dutch colony, were published in the Netherlands as a guide for other Seceders who were considering the voyage.[3] These letters contain much sensible advice:

> I want to warn each of you against Ellinckhuijzen and his partner who, speaking Dutch and posing as friends, are in reality the greatest of frauds. I can not emphasize enough that you should learn English. In knowing that you will be bringing a treasure with you. How often I have felt sorry for a person who looked as though he were not possessed of his reason and was openly cheated without being aware of it. One learns quickly from an experience like that. Anyone who has learned English in the Netherlands need not be surprised if, at first, he understands little of what is said here, for the accent here is strange; however, one soon becomes accustomed to it — sometimes within a half hour, as was the case with myself. All American industries are on a large scale, and I can say from experience that bread is to be found here; nay, more than bread for all who will work.[4]

Among the most interesting letters are those which tell of the van Malsens' experiences during their journey to America:

> Once we saw an iceberg of unbelievable size, a floating mass. Sometimes fish as large as horses, etc. It was wonderful for me to see the effervescent sea appear at night as though it were fire, due to phosphorescent action. One night we saw the northern lights above Jupiter; the first mate, who was with me, had never seen it so beautiful.[5]

Cornelis van Malsen also wrote about working and living conditions in the Dutch colony:

> There is much joy among the people at being free from the persecutions found in the Netherlands and also because it is so easy to obtain bread. Insofar as is possible I hope to inaugurate plans to bring some of my poor and believing friends here.
> How tragic it is to endure poverty in the Netherlands, while here all nature is waiting for people .... One need not worry about trouble here; employment can be found immediately both in and outside of our colony.[6]

Such enthusiastic letters from Michigan, written by the van Malsens and other immigrants, were an important factor in encouraging thousands of other Seceders to leave the Netherlands and travel to a new home in America.

5

Captain Henry Van Allen and Peter Frederick Verhoeff

Among those involved in transporting the thousands of immigrants bound for the American west was Captain Henry Van Allen, a lakeboat captain of Netherlandic origin. Son of a Loyalist family from New York State, Van Allen and his brother John played an important role in the commercial development of Windsor. Although he did not live in Essex County, he was active as a shipbuilder and mariner. His brother John did live in Sandwich Township, and was active for several years as a businessman in the Detroit River region.

The Van Allen family was originally from the city of Utrecht. About 1650 two brothers, Pieter and Laurens van Alen, left for New Netherland where they settled on Long Island. Several generations later, a member of this family, Jacob Van Allen, came to Upper Canada and settled with other Loyalists in Matilda Township of Dundas County. One of his sons Henry Van Allen moved to Woodhouse in Norfolk County about 1795, where on 25 December 1795 he married Winnifred Rapelje, daughter of his new business partner Abraham A. Rapelje. From 1795 to 1800 the two families conducted business near Port Dover. Later, Van Allen participated in the War of 1812, and his father-in-law served as a captain.[1]

In 1833, Henry and Winnifred's son, also named Henry Van Allen, took up farming on the Thames River near the growing settlement of Chatham, which by this time had overtaken Dolsen's in importance. There he owned a farm of 100 acres, with about thirty cleared, lying on the river.

Van Allen improved his land and quickly became a prominent businessman. He married Elizabeth McGregor, daughter of important mill-owner John McGregor, who had settled in 1781 on the Thames. The McGregors and Van Allens soon became even more closely related, as Elizabeth McGregor's brother Duncan married Henry Van Allen's sister Cynthia. The close connection with the McGregor family, whose members retained their social and business connections with Essex County, meant that the Van Allens also established business ties there. The new family venture in Essex County, established in the 1830s, was in the hands of Henry Van Allen's brother John, and consisted of a store, house, shop, and wharf on the riverfront in the hamlet of Windsor.

Henry Van Allen went into business in Chatham with his brother-in-law Duncan, and they turned their attention to shipbuilding. By this time, the sailing vessels of the Thames were being converted to steam, the first completed in 1832. One year later, this McGregor-Van Allen partnership built two steamships, the *Thames* and the *Cynthia*.

The *Thames* weighed 160 tonnes with a 37-metre deck, a 24-metre promenade, and a six-metre beam. The gentlemen's cabin sported 22 permanent and 18 movable berths. Fitted in Cleveland with a 45-horsepower engine, she operated from 1833 to 1838 primarily between Chatham, Buffalo, and Windsor.

The ferry service was in heavy use. According to the Sandwich *Western Herald* of 13 November 1838, emigration to the west of the United States by way of Buffalo and Detroit during 1836 averaged about 1,000 a day, most people going by way of Lake Erie.[2] About 400 a day made the journey eastward from Detroit to Buffalo.[3] By December 1836, 30 steamboats "of the first and second classes", and 150 sailing-vessels, plied between Detroit and Buffalo. The Sandwich ferry was exceedingly busy: per month "an average of two hundred wagons, 150 pairs of horses, two hundred pairs of oxen, and eight hundred persons with their moveables", came through Canada and crossed at Detroit during seven months of the year 1836.[4] By 1838 the steamboats left Chatham three times a week, carrying emigrants and their baggage to the ferry at Sandwich. The *Thames* was in service as one of these Chatham steamboats for five years, from 1833 until 4 December 1838. On that day it burned as it lay moored, loaded with ammunition, at Van Allen's wharf in Windsor. It had become a target for the attacking "Patriots" in the one-day Battle of Windsor.

The incendiarists were members of the Patriot Club of Detroit, men who sympathized with the Reformers attempting to overthrow the government of Upper Canada. They announced their plan to liberate the province from British control and make it part of the United States. On 4 December 1838 about 150 men came from Detroit on the steamer *Champlain*, landing on the Pilette farm to the east of Windsor. They shot at the barrack, a yellow two-storey frame house which had been commandeered by the Essex Militia. It caught fire and was destroyed.

On the bend of the river almost directly in front of the burning guardhouse was the steamer *Thames*, tied up at Van Allen's wharf. It too was set afire in a deliberate act of reprisal, for only a year before the British had burned an American ship, the *Caroline*, at Niagara.

An eyewitness of the Windsor attack, Victor Ouellette, describes another act of vandalism:

> I was thirteen years of age at this time and was sent by my father, Jean Baptiste, with my mother to Sandwich. On our way we met three or four companies of volunteers on their way to Windsor, and a little later Colonel Prince on horseback, dressed in his shooting coat and with a large coonskin cap on his head. My brother Denis was clerking in Berhoeff's [sic] store, on the river bank, just opposite where Glengarry Avenue now is. The brigands entered the store and helped themselves to what they wanted, but my brother was not harmed.[5]

The store was not Berhoeff's but Peter Frederick Verhoeff's, founded by him and George Jasperson. It escaped destruction probably because its owner was well known as a merchant on the frontier, and carried on business on both sides of the border.

The Patriots, meanwhile, finally encountered the defending force led by Col. Prince and later strengthened by British troops from Amherstburg. They engaged in a bloody battle in Col. Baby's pear orchard. While reports of the day's losses differ, it appears that about 32 Patriots were killed and an equal number taken prisoner. Some were later hanged, while others were deported to Van Diemen's Land.

Peter F. Verhoeff had emigrated from the Netherlands to New York State as a young man. He arrived in Detroit about 1826 or 1827, joining in a business partnership with Peter F. Brakeman of Detroit and George Jasperson, a German-speaking Dane from Schleswig-Holstein who had immigrated to America some years before and had first settled in Lewisburg, Ohio, before moving to Detroit.

He and his partners were able to take advantage of rapidly improving communications with their suppliers in Montreal and New York. The fur trade, which had been such a profitable source of income to traders such as Dolsen, was coming to an end, but there was now the opportunity to build a lucrative business as supplier of goods to immigrants passing through or settling in the border regions.

For some time, Verhoeff's and Jasperson's firm had two establishments, one on each side of the Detroit River.[6] The Detroit store was located on the riverfront lot originally belonging to the Antoine Beaubien farm of the old French settlement. The Canadian store was at the eastern end of Sandwich Township.

By December 1830 both Jasperson and Verhoeff had officially taken up residence in Sandwich Township to qualify as landed immigrants, and to the right to own Canadian property on the Canadian side. However, it was not until 13 April 1835 that they finally sold their Detroit holdings to Francis Dwight and emigrated to the Canadian side of the river. George Jasperson remained in Canada for some years, founding a well-known Essex County family, the Jaspersons of Kingsville. He later returned to the United States to live there permanently. Verhoeff bought Jasperson's share of the Windsor business and remained its owner for more than 20 years. Eventually, he also returned to America.

When Verhoeff and Jasperson first extended

their Detroit commercial operations to the Canadian side (about 1828 or 1829), they did not formally petition for ownership of the Sandwich Township property. They remedied this on 3 December 1830, for other merchants were beginning to offer competition. They successfully petitioned for ownership of lot number 87 in the first concession of the Township of Sandwich in the Western District of the Province of Upper Canada.

Verhoeff's chief rival was James Dougall, an immigrant from Paisley, Scotland, and there is some doubt as to which one set up business first. The two men started at about the same time and were definitely competitors.

Dougall announced in 1831 in the *Canadian Emigrant* that he dealt in British goods, and listed a surprisingly fine line of imports, including

> a superb assortment of Brussels, superfine and fine Kidderminster, Scotch, and Venetian carpeting ... seven kinds of tea, twenty kegs best loch-fine Herrings, and two hampers of Cheshire cheese.

Verhoeff's advertisement appeared on the same page as Dougall's:

> Shovels and Spades
> Brass candlesticks
> Scythes and Sickles, Pinchers
> Knippers, large Pearl Buttons
> Table and Tea-spoons, &&&
> Comprising almost every article necessary for the Western Market....[7]

By comparison, his stock seems plainer than Dougall's but Verhoeff also states that he will accept "Cash or Produce"; also that "the attention of Country Dealers is particularly invited". It would seem that the two rival merchants were trying to reach a somewhat different clientelle.

Some of Dougall's customers came from Detroit to shop at his store since it was conveniently close to the Ferry; others came from the newly established Scotch Settlement on Lake St. Clair. By the time that Verhoeff's store was involved in the Battle of Windsor, Dougall had a far larger and more successful establishment.

Another store was to be found at Van Allen's wharf. This was probably set up in 1833 and was kept by John Van Allen until the fall of 1840 when the following advertisement appeared in the *Western Herald and Farmer's Magazine*:

> To Rent: the Store House, Shop and Wharf, together with the Premises thereto belonging, lately occupied by John Vanallen, situate in Windsor.[8]

Even though Henry Van Allen's ship had been burned by the Patriots, he continued to serve as a lakeboat captain, making his home in Chatham. His name was frequently mentioned in the *Canadian Emigrant* (published in Sandwich). He became captain of the *Kent*, which made its first trip from Chatham down the lakes to Buffalo in the spring of 1842.

On this occasion, he received a testimonial from his passengers, one of which was printed in the Chatham *Journal* of 21 May, 1842. In it, reference was made to the "clean, comfortable, and well-arranged arrangements". The authors added:

> To yourself, who is so well and favorably known to the travelling community, we need scarcely say anything were it not in justice to the owners who in the appointment of you as Master have, we think, consulted as well their own interests as that of the passengers, while your studious endeavor at all times to please will contribute in no small degree to enhance the advantages of a boat on our side of the lake.[9]

In thanking the authors of this tribute, Van Allen replied:

> I now pledge my word to you, gentlemen, and the public, as long as I have the honor of commanding this boat, my anxious desire will be to make her profitable to her owners and a source of accomodation to all who may favor me with their business.[10]

The *Kent* was one of the comfortable boats which had been built in Chatham for the Great Lakes. Unfortunately, after the fine maiden voyage and exchange of compliments, a controversy arose in which Captain Van Allen played a major role. In the pages of the Sandwich *Herald*, he later wrote a series of strongly-worded letters in which he condemned another ship, H.M.S. *Minos*, for not coming to the aid of the *Kent* when it was disabled three kilometres offshore from Port Colborne. In one of these letters he accused that the *Minos*:

> positively refused to tow us [the *Kent*] in, although at the time they had nothing to do; and obliged me, at the imminent risk of the boat, to travel twenty-two miles through the mud to Buffalo, and employ an American steamer to take us down, and enable us to get our damage repaired! Treatment such as this I think is unprecedented, and justly merits the censure of the public as well as the government which they profess to serve .... I shall not forget to report this matter to the proper quarter; and in the mean time shall not fail to let owners and masters of vessels know what they have to expect from Her Majesty's steamer *Minos* in case they should be as unfortunately situated as myself.[11]

What actually happened is not fully known, but it is certain that public sympathy was on Captain Van Allen's side. (The *Kent* capsized in Lake Erie three years later, on 12 August 1845, when she collided with the steamer *London*. Sixteen lives were lost in the accident.)

The entire Van Allen family seems to have been interested in ships and shipping, for several members were involved. Among these was Captain Henry Van Allen's nephew Daniel Ross Van Allen, a close business associate. In fact, Daniel Ross Van Allen had moved with his uncle from Port Dover to Chatham when a young boy of ten. He began his business career as a clerk and quickly rose to become one of the leading mill-owners and shipbuilders of the area. He built sawmills on the river flats just east of the Chatham town limits, near his ship building works, and in 1858 built the Chatham sawmill. Not long afterwards, he bought a sawmill in Belle River in Essex County, which was to play a role in the Van Orden murder case of 1868.

During the 1840s and early 1850s, meanwhile, Peter Frederick Verhoeff continued to do business from his general store. In 1849 he was one of a delegation of grateful Windsor citizens who made an official visit to Detroit to thank the Fire Brigade for coming to the rescue of Windsor on the night of April 6. Friend Palmer, the Detroit historian, described the disastrous fire of that night, which caused an estimated $35,000 worth of damage to Windsor:

Big Fire In Windsor
In 1849, while Mr. Duncan was chief engineer of the Volunteer Fire Department, a fire broke out in Windsor on the night of April 6, and as far as appearances from this side indicated, the City of Windsor was in danger of being wiped out by fire. Dougall's large brick store on the west side of Ferry Street and abutting on the river, was a mass of flames and a high wind was prevailing. After a delay of an hour and a half, owing to the absence of the ferry boat, Duncan was enabled to send only one engine (No.5) across, and that was by a small steam boat called the *Hastings*, that he happened to see make a landing at the foot of Shelby Street. The reason why only one engine was sent across the river was owing to the smallness of the *Hastings*. Duncan, however, at the timely suggestion of Mr. John Owen, took over at the same time 250 feet additional of hose, which addition saved the City of Windsor many, many thousands of dollars.

When Chief Duncan and his men reached the scene nearly an acre of territory had been burned, and the northwest wind was sending a mass of cinders and flame directly towards the large frame hotel known as the Windsor Castle, which stood directly opposite the site of the present Crawford House.

About two hours and a half after the landing of the boat, the Detroit firemen being augmented in the meantime, by the arrival of Engine Company No. 2, on board the steamer *Ariel*, the flames were subdued, the fire completely checked. It was a fierce, stubborn fight.[12]

While James Dougall's store was lost in the fire, Peter Frederick Verhoeff's was saved, as were those of two other Windsor merchants. In gratitude, "during and after the fire the Windsor people entertained the Detroit firemen in royal fashion, providing an abundance of food, hot coffee and other drinkables, with all the cigars they could utilize, and on our departure they cheered us most loyally".[13]

The day after the fire, Verhoeff was among the grateful Windsorites who met at the Windsor Castle Hotel and approved the making of plans for a further expression of thanks to the Detroit Fire Department, which was under the direction of James Van Dyke, a Detroit voluntary fireman and prominent lawyer of Dutch origin. Three months later, in early July, Verhoeff and other Windsor businessmen and officials made a formal visit to Detroit, landing at the foot of Woodward Avenue. There the delegation was met by the Detroit firemen, drawn up in a hollow square to receive the Canadians. Lively music by a German band added to the festivities. The Canadian delegation, headed by the Honourable Arthur Rankin as Chairman, made a presentation to the Detroit Fire Brigade of a silver trumpet, beautifully engraved with the coat of arms of the United States on one side, that of Great Britain on the other. Between the two coats-of-arms was engraved a picture of an antique fire engine, a goose-neck hand engine of a type used in the earliest days of firefighting in Detroit at the beginning of the nineteenth century. The trumpet carried the inscription:

> Presented: to the Fire Brigade of Detroit, by the inhabitants of Windsor and Sandwich, as a testimonial of their gratitude for their noble and generous conduct in crossing the river, under the direction of Mr. Duncan, the Chief Engineer, during the intensely cold night of the 6th of April, 1849, with their engines, by means of which, under their able and unwearied exertions and management, the total destruction of the Village of Windsor by fire was mainly prevented.[14]

The trumpet was presented by the Honourable Arthur Rankin to James Van Dyke. At the conclusion of the ceremony, the officials from both sides of the Detroit River and the firemen of Detroit went to the National Hotel for a formal banquet.

This was one of the last local events in which Verhoeff played a role, for a year later he sold his store and other properties in Windsor. Some months later, he left for Staten Island in New York State where he took up residence. Although he purchased land in Detroit in 1855, he was content to merely correspond with his former business associates of Windsor and Detroit from his new home in Staten Island.[15]

It is apparent that settlers of Dutch heritage who arrived in the early part of the nineteenth century tended to be active in business, both as merchants and shipbuilders. This trend continued in the second part of the century. H.A. Vanavery opened the "Great Cash Store", a general store in South Woodslee. Daniel Ross Van Allen, Captain Van Allen's nephew, bought a sawmill in Belle River, a newly developing community in the 1850s and 1860s. Another mill there was bought by Abraham Van Orden, an American of Dutch ancestry from New York State. Their sawmills cut lumber for the American market, as well as for local residents, while their gristmills ground the grain.

The Vanavery general store in South Woodslee was typical of many of the small Essex County stores of the late nineteenth century. *It provided a varied stock of commonly needed supplies for sale to residents of the hamlet and the surrounding area. Like others of its kind, this store also served a social function as a meeting place where news was exchanged. The Vanavery family was of United Empire Loyalist origin.*

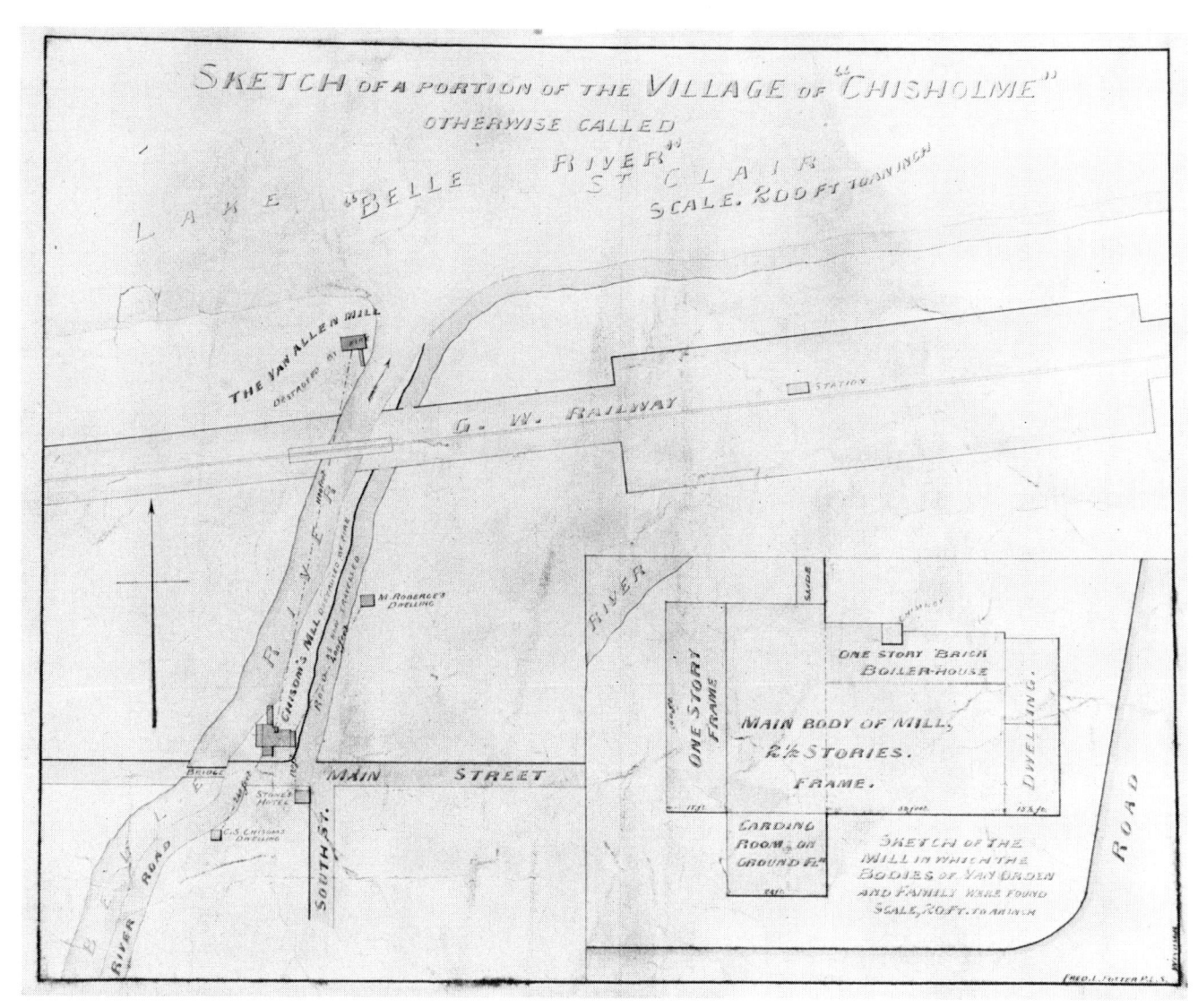

This sketch of the mill in which the Van Orden family lost their lives on 30 August 1868, was prepared as evidence for the autumn Essex assizes, which began in the Sandwich Court House on Tuesday, 10 November 1868. *Other than this sketch, now in the Hiram Walker Museum of Windsor, there are no longer any official records of the fire and the ensuing investigations and murder trial. The Van Allen Mill, seen in the upper left of the sketch, also burned on the same day. It belonged to Daniel Ross Van Allen of Chatham, a descendant of the Loyalist family of Van Allens, a number of whose members had business interests in Essex County during the nineteenth century.*

6

Murder In The Mill

In less than two decades the hamlet of Windsor, so hopelessly unprogressive in the eyes of Mrs. Jameson in 1837, became a prosperous commercial centre. It had grown from a small settlement of 200 to nearly four times that size at the time of its incorporation as a village in 1854, and had doubled in size again by 1858 when it was incorporated as a town. Essex County, which had been an isolated, largely rural area with only three settlements of any size, quickly became settled by new immigrants who claimed the best of the arable land and founded a number of small communities.

This flurry of activity was caused by the arrival of the Great Western Railway in 1854, an event which marked the beginning of a new and progressive era for Windsor. The first passenger train from Niagara Falls arrived on 17 January 1854. Soon, every day brought trains filled with passengers, many of whom boarded the railroad's ferry ship. They would remain on board overnight, and the next day be ferried across to Detroit, to resume their journey. With some exceptions, most of the travellers were immigrants on their way to the American midwest, including Dutch bound for the Holland, Michigan settlement founded by Van Raalte.

One of these Dutch travellers has left an account of his trip which shows that he thought he had already arrived in Detroit when his train drew into the Windsor station. Evert Wonnink, travelling in May 1871 from Geesteren in the Netherlands to Grand Rapids, via Liverpool and Quebec, wrote home to a friend:

> We stayed in Quebec until four in the afternoon, then went onto the train, and went quickly on, night and day. Wednesday morning at seven o'clock we arrived in Montreal, which is a beautiful city with lovely meadows. Just before Montreal we went over a large railway bridge,[1] completely closed overhead like a tunnel.... Almost everywhere the Railroad runs through great woods, although in some places one also finds beautiful meadows and farmland. Everywhere men stand upright while chopping down the trees, so tremendous stumps remain, a full ell[2] high above ground. All the wood is burned here; oh! if you could have it in Holland! You travel for hours alongside piles of sawn wood, for the locomotives are stoked with wood here. At last we came to Detroit, where we arrived on Thursday evening, and were at a

standstill until morning, when we were taken over the water and at noon our journey to Grand Rapids was recommenced. At seven o'clock on Saturday morning the word "Grand Rapids" was called out by the conductor, a happy sound to our ears! Here we stepped out and said farewell to the many Dutch fellow travellers with whom we had made acquaintance.[3]

Providing the necessary services and supplies for travellers passing through the town and for those who settled in the area brought new prosperity to Windsor, especially its hotels and taverns. At this point, a new type of immigrant began to arrive as well: the labourer who worked on the railroads and in the small communities developing along them. Earlier in the nineteenth century, the population was mostly rural. Even those living in Windsor tended to be self-sufficient (although some of the French farmwives near the border occasionally took surplus produce to Detroit by ferry to sell it at the old Berthelet Market). But with the growth of new communities in the middle of the century, the population became more varied both in background and occupation. English, Irish, and Scottish immigrants arrived in number; a stream of Black immigrants arrived, escaping from slavery in the United States; German immigrants, together with a few of other nationalities of Europe, began to trickle into the county. With its border position and prosperity Windsor attracted a particularly sizeable group of American immigrants.

Among the new American immigrants was a real estate dealer from New York, Charles S. Chisom. In 1863, he settled on property he had bought earlier in the Police Village of Rochester, now Belle River. Belle River was then in the earliest stages of growth, but held promise for the future.

Between 1850 and 1867, British immigrants began to move into the village to join the French Canadians who had lived in the area for years and had formed the nucleus of the county's population. Soon Charles Chisom had added many village lots and farm properties, particularly on the north side of the new line of the Great Western Railway, which passed through the village. He also owned property on both sides of Tecumseh Road, and a large part of the eastern end of the village. He had become powerful and influential, and held a number of positions in local government. He even succeeded in having the "Police Village of Rochester" resurveyed and its name changed to "the Village of Chisholme" in 1857, although the name later became Belle River.[4]

During the ten-year period from 1857 to 1867, Chisom obtained a gristmill and a sawmill to add to his holdings. The new mills were most important to the economy of the growing village, and were remarked upon by a traveller of the 1850s who described

> the thriving village of Belle River, only a few years past a dense forest, but now showing every sign of life and activity. The large saw and grist mills in operation deprive it of its otherwise rustic appearance and the shrill whistle of the locomotive as it drives up to the station, makes one forget that he is far away in the woods. Having refreshed the inner man at Stone's Hotel, which by the way is no mean establishment, we were rather agreeably surprised to find such good fare.[5]

One of the most tragic events in local history occurred in Belle River on Sunday, 30 August 1868 when two steam sawmills caught fire, and foul play was suspected. The blazes proved to be the work of an arsonist. The mystery deepened as the bodies of three individuals were found — previously murdered.

It is clear that the events which led to the murders coincided with the arrival of an American businessman from Chicago, Abraham Van Orden, who came to Belle River with his wife and teenaged grandson in January 1868.

Van Orden was a member of the Van Orden family of Greene County, New York. Their immigrant ancestor was Pieter Claesen Van Norden, thought to have come to New Amsterdam from Norden (near Putten) in Gelderland, the Northern Netherlands, in the middle of the seventeenth century. In the early nineteenth century, several members of this large family migrated to the midwestern states. Abraham moved to Chicago, and later to Detroit. (A brother went to Toledo, Ohio). By the time Van Orden arrived in Belle River he was about 50 years old. He had left a successful business career in Chicago and brought a considerable amount of money with him, intending to settle in a small Canadian community. Van Orden was soon negotiating to buy Chisom's mill. Apparently a satisfactory bargain was struck, for Van Orden and his family moved to Belle River shortly thereafter.

Although the case was a sensational one, no court records remain extant other than the map drawn for use at the trial.[6] The only source of information about the case is provided by newspaper accounts of the period, particularly the seemingly verbatim report of the evidence taken before the coroner, and published in the Chatham *Weekly Planet*.

In its headlines of 3 September 1868, the *Planet* reported:

Dreadful Catastrophe at Belle River!

Two Steam Saw Mills Burned
and three Human Lives Lost!

A Man, His Wife and Grandson Burned!

Undoubted Incendiarism
and Supposed Triple Murder

Coroner's Inquest Today!

One of the most lamentable, and disastrous events

which ever transpired in this section of the country, occurred at Belle River on the line of the Great Western Railway, on Sunday morning last, whereby three estimable human beings were lost and large and valuable properties destroyed. From a personal visit to the scene of these disasters, we have been able to collect the following reliable facts in relation to them. It seems that a fire was first discovered issuing from the Northwest side of the Belle River Saw and Grist Mill, an establishment which had been doing a large local business for a great number of years. Of course the discovery of this fire soon aroused the villagers, and confusion, and excitement seemed to possess one and all. Without delay every effort that could be made was made to save the burning building, but the hour — about half past 12 o'clock — at which the fire broke out, and the limited resources at the command of the people, precluded all hope of saving the mill or any portion of it. It being old and extremely dry, and, besides, being surrounded by all sorts of inflammable rubbish, the entire structure was speedily wrapped in one sheet of hissing, cracking, roaring flame, which greatly endangered a large portion of the main buildings in the village. In the midst of the prevailing excitement a new cause for consideration presented itself, which threw, if possible, additional dismay into the treaty, of the inhabitants of Belle River — this was the painful revelation of the fact that another steam Saw mill in the place was also on fire! This mill was the new one erected in the winter of 1866 & '67 at the mouth of Belle River on the west side, and owned by D. R. Van Allen, Esq., of Chatham, and worked by Messrs. Marshall and Brown of Detroit. To this new scene of destruction some 60 rods from the former many of the villagers hastened, and with a limited supply of pails were enabled to save a considerable quantity of lumber, the property of Mr. Van Allen; but we are sorry to say that Messrs. Marshall and Brown lost several piles of lumber which had been cut for the Detroit Market. This mill, it at once became apparent, it, must have been set on fire by an incendiary, from the fact that it was seen to burn on the south east corner, in a distant portion of the mill from where the boiler and engine were located. And, moreover, a passer by discovered in the vicinity not far from where the fire was first seen, a jug which, it was quite evident, had but a short time before contained a quantity of Kerosene oil. This was about a quarter to 1 o'clock a.m. The Belle River Mill was a mass of burning ruins. It then flashed through the minds of some persons to enquire where Mr. Van Orden who worked the mill, and family, who, it was known, occupied a portion of the Belle River Mill, were.

A search of the ruins of the mill led to the discovery of the bodies of Abraham Van Orden, his wife Elizabeth, and his 15-year-old grandson James.

After a vivid description of the search of the ruins and the discovery of the bodies, the journalist continues:

Of course, a coroner was at once sent for, and at an early hour Dr. E. B. Donnelly, of Windsor, was at the scene of the fearful disaster, and a jury was summoned today (Monday) when Dr. Casgrain will appear to give medical testimony. That both these mills were set on fire by some evil disposed person, there appears to be not a shadow of doubt, and, more horrible than all, it seems to be most indelibly and to us reasonably, too — impressed on the minds of the inhabitants of Belle River, that a triple murder was previously foully perpetrated! The basis of this theory is as follows: Mr. Van Orden had been at Windsor on the previous Saturday, where he was engaged in an arbitration concerning the possession of the Belle River mills. In the afternoon of that day, he returned home by the train, and it is known that he brought with him a considerable sum of money — how much it is not said. — but it is a fact, we believe, that evening he showed some $500 in silver to one man, and, before leaving Windsor, had lent a quantity of money to another person. Then, just before the first fire broke out, three or four distinct pistol shots were heard in the vicinity of the mill by several persons, and a few minutes later a person was seen behind the mill. This was about midnight. A little after the mill was on fire. After the Belle River Mill began to burn, a watchman was on duty at Van Allen's Mill, came over to the Belle River Mill, and a few minutes later still the same man who it is said was seen behind the Belle River Mill, was noticed going along the road on the west side of the river, and in five minutes more Van Allen's mill was a blaze! And more, after the fire the ruins were searched for $500 which it was known Mr. Van Orden had come home with; but none of this money was found — only a few dollars, some ten or fifteen, being removed from the ashes in the vicinity of where the miller had deposited that amount during the previous day. Now what did Mr. Van Orden do with the $500? What were the three or four pistol shots for? And more strange then all, how was it that not one of the Van Ordens, if not killed, did not leave the building, or show themselves at the windows — which were open, before or when the fire reached them, which it must have taken some minutes to do, from the time it began or even from the time it was first seen by the villagers? The painful conclusion forces itself upon our mind, as well as it has forced itself upon the minds of the inhabitants of Belle River, that a hellish triple murder was first committed, followed by a robbery, and the whole of a series of damnable crimes, wound up by a double incendiarism, whereby the three dead bodies of the unfortunate Van Ordens were consumed along with two valuable steam saw mills! Should these surmises turn out to be correct, hanging, drawing, and quartering would be too mild treatment for the hellish perpetrator of such a fearful catalogue of guilt. Meantime, we await the result of the investigation, which we sincerely trust will be searching and severe.[7]

On September 10 in the next issue of the *Weekly Planet*, the Chatham reporter continued his report with a detailed account of the evidence taken before the coroners Dr. Donnelly and Dr. Casgrain, who met early on the day immediately following the fire. In the meantime on Sunday, jurymen had been summoned. Immediately on arrival in Belle River at 8:15 on Monday morning, the Windsor doctors went to Stone's Hotel, the "Rochester House" to swear in the jurymen.

It took three days to collect all the evidence. Chisom was recalled on the third day for further questioning, and it appeared that the sale of the mill to Van Orden had been most irregular:

> (Chisom): Witness owned the Belle River mill; sold it to Van Orden on the 20th January, and bought it back again in the last of March, closing the bargain on the 3rd day of April. Van Orden commenced a suit in Chancery and the whole matter referred to arbitration, which had not yet been settled upon the award, but both met on Saturday and felt satisfied on how it would go, and witness borrowed some money from the deceased, for his witness, wife, and agreed to treat the deceased as a man.

> (A witness, Ansel B. Graham of Windsor): Said he knew the late Mr. Van Orden well, saw him last on Saturday at Windsor, engaged in an arbitration case with Chisom, witness, Mr. Shipley and Mr. Cotter being the arbitrators. Captain Robarsh [*sic*] was also in Windsor at the same time, a witness on the arbitration case. Robarsh and Van Orden did not meet in witness' presence, neither did Robarsh exhibit in giving his testimony, any friendly feeling towards Van Orden. Robarsh said he went in with Van Orden determined to beat Chisom thought Van Orden a decent man, but found out he was a d---n old scoundrel, would not do as he agreed to with him, and then he, Robarsh, turned to Chisom to help him, Chisom, to beat Van Orden. The arbitration is not yet settled. Both Van Orden and Chisom claimed to own the mill, and the whole question of ownership and indebtedness connected with the mill was before the arbitrators. Van Orden claimed the mill in lieu of the non-fulfillment of agreement made on the part of Chisom, who claimed the mill back and $2,000 damages.[8]

It appeared that Chisom had taken out $2,000 worth of insurance on the mill. Another witness, John S. Armour, had heard Roberge make threats

> that he would clear Van Orden out of the place; also hear him say that he would grease the railway track the length of his farm and set fire to the railway bridge if the company did not pay him ... Witness had heard Robarts say, between three and four weeks ago, to Chisom, "the best thing you can do with the mill is to insure it and set fire to it." ... People in general have not much confidence in Robarsh; when in liquor he is regarded as a very dangerous man.[9]

On the final day, a statement by Roberge was read. It began:

> I am brought here innocently; am as innocent as the angels above me. The generality of the public are down upon me without just cause and provocation, but I hope to prove myself innocent. Last spring I was arrested for setting fire to the Rail Road Bridge, which was untrue. Last summer, as you all know, a horse and cow died on my premises, and I was accused of killing them, which proves there is a conspiracy against me. I am as innocent as the angels above, of the charge against me.[10]

At the end of the third day, a verdict was given:

> That one Moses Robarsh, on the night of the 29th day of August, between the hours of eleven of the clock p.m., and one of the clock, a.m., on the thirtieth of August, of the year aforesaid, in the County of Essex, did feloniously, wilfully and of malice aforethought, kill and murder one Abraham Van Orden, by causing him to be burned to death in a room of a mill in which he, the said Abraham Van Orden, slept, by setting fire to the said mill, against the peace of our Lady the Queen, her crown and dignity. And the jurors aforesaid, upon their oath aforesaid, further say, that Charles S. Chisom, before the said felony was committed, to wit, on the night of the 29th day of August, in the year aforesaid, feloniously and maliciously did incite, move, procure, aid, counsel, hire and command the said Moses Robarsh to do and commit against the peace of our Lady the Queen, her crown and dignity. In Witness, & etc.[11]

Roberge and Chisom were arrested, and feelings in the village ran high, for the Van Ordens appear to have had good friends and neighbours who threatened to lynch "the guilty parties". The third day of the preliminary investigation, when the verdict was reached, many villagers signed a petition which was handed to John O'Connor, Member of Parliament. This stated their disgust and strong disapproval that he would agree to be the defense lawyer for the two prisoners. However, the *Planet* told its readers that such a display of feeling was untoward, for under British justice everyone had the right to a fair trial.

At the Essex Assizes of autumn 1868, which began on Tuesday, November 10, Roberge and Chisom were found not guilty. In November, 1869 the Essex County Council offered a reward of $400, and the township councils of Maidstone and Rochester each $100, for the discovery of the murderer or murderers of the Van Orden family and the incendiarists who set fire to the Belle River mills.

Chisom continued to be active in real estate dealings in Belle River and Rochester, and was a wealthy and powerful local figure until nearly the end of the century. The murderers of the Van Orden family were never officially brought to justice.

7

Descendants of the Loyalists

During the early part of the nineteenth century, new settlers came into the county as roads were built to make the interior accessible. It was not until the 1820s that the ridge leading into Leamington was settled. This area was opened as Talbot Road West, and was developed through Ruthven, Cottam, Essex, and Maidstone towards the town of Sandwich. By mid-century most of the county was open for settlement and the harsh conditions of pioneer life had become greatly alleviated. The small log houses were giving way to larger frame buildings, many of them still to be seen in Essex County today. Tecumseh Road opened up another part of the county in 1838, bringing in more settlers and developers. Completion of the Great Western Railway to Windsor in 1854 assured the place of Windsor as the largest centre of population in the county.

In the early 1870s another railway was completed: the Canada Southern, constructed between the Niagara and Detroit Rivers. This line, later to become part of the New York Central system, had connections with the United States at each end. It cut diagonally across the county from Tilbury to Gordon (close to Amherstburg), and opened up still other parts of the interior to lumbering and farming. Comber, Woodslee, and Essex Centre were situated along the line and grew quickly as a result. By the end of the century, the forests in the interior were largely cleared, and little unsettled land remained.

A third railway was built in the 1880s: the Lake Erie, Essex and Detroit River Railway, constructed by the Walker family for business purposes. It brought prosperity to the South Essex centres of Leamington, Kingsville and Harrow, among other communities.

(The last railway to reach Essex County was the Canadian Pacific, in 1890. This event was of unusual importance for it brought the new industry of salt mining to Windsor. The arrival of the CPR and its significance will be given further consideration in the next chapter).

Among the many British, American, and Canadian settlers who poured into the county to take up land made accessible by the new railways were some of the descendants of the Loyalists, including a number of Dutch origin. Among these were several members of the Van Atter family, formerly of Wellington

County, who moved in mid-century to the new town of Leamington. A branch of the Van Buskirk family moved to Essex County from Shelburne, Nova Scotia, where a Loyalist ancestor had settled. A granddaughter of Colonel Vrooman of Butler's Rangers, who had been living at Queenston, married an Amherstburg doctor of German extraction, Dr. Oscar Teeter, and came to live in Essex County. Members of the Van Every family arrived in mid-century from Flamboro West and Dumfries. Still other members of this large family came from Niagara. The Van Horns from Adolphustown, the Van Kleeks from Hawkesbury and Vankleek Hill, and the Van Sickles from Ancaster were all represented in the county by the 1800s.

One of the largest of these families, represented in several of the new communities, was the Van Every family, originally from New York State. The name was spelled in various ways, including Vanevery, Vanavery, Van Avery, and in the seventeenth century in New York State, van Iveren and van Jeverden. A few of the Essex County representatives of this family were not the descendants of Loyalist members of the family, but of American branches. These immigrants came to Essex County directly from the United States, some of them from Detroit where Peter Van Every had settled in the eighteenth century. However, most of the Essex County members of the family were descendants of a Loyalist from Scohary, New York, named McGregor Van Every, who died at Niagara in 1786. On 15 May 1788, his eldest son David Van Every gave evidence before the Loyalist Commissioners[1] at Montreal, making a claim for his late father who had died two years earlier leaving a wife and seven children. David Van Every stated:

> His Father joined the British Army in 1781. Five of his son [sic] were in the King's service from the first of the War. His father attempted to join the Army early but was seized and imprisoned. He was always friendly to Gt. Britain.
> His mother tells him they lost 2 Horses, and 2 Cows and some young Cattle, farming utensils and Furniture. All these were taken from them on acct. of their Loyalty.
> Mary Van Every, Wid. of Claimt., says her husband lost 2 Horses, 4 Cows, furniture, and farming utensils. Her Husband was six months in Gaol.
> Capt. John McDonnel, of Butler's Rangers, says that McGregor Van Every and five of his sons served in the same Corps with him. They were all Loyal people.
> Mary Van Every lived always as Claimt.'s Wife and mother to the children.[2]

The Van Every family of New York State was descended from a pioneer settler of New Netherland, Myndert Frederickse van Every. An American scholar believes the family came from Jeveren in Oldenburg.[3] However, the Van Every family of Ontario has carried out research in the Netherlands which leads it to believe that the ancestors came from a small community in the province of Zeeland. This hamlet is named Everinghe and is in the township of Ellewoudsdijk in South Beveland.[4]

According to family tradition, the father, Fredericke van Iveren, remained in the Netherlands as did his son Rynier, who acted as an agent in Amsterdam for his two brothers Myndert and Carsten when they emigrated to America about 1653. The immigrants were master smiths who played a prominent role in the settlement of the Dutch colony at Beverwyck (later called Albany). The brothers were Lutheran at a time when the state religion of New Netherland was Reformed. In 1675, after the English had captured New Netherland, Myndert and four other Lutherans sent a petition to the governor general asking to exercise "their religious worship without let or hindrance".[5] The request was granted "on condition they conduct themselves peaceably without giving offence to the reformed religion which is the state church".[6] In 1680 the land on which the Lutheran church of Beverwyck had been built was declared "fully paid for, the first penny with the last", and deeded to Myndert as elder, Carston as deacon, and two others, "to do with and dispose of as they might do with their own patrimonial estate, being for the use of the whole church".[7]

McGregor van Every, the ancestor of the Canadian branch of the family, was an elderly man when he arrived as a Loyalist in Niagara. He was a descendant of Myndert van Iversen and was born in Arents (later Orange), New York on 27 April 1723. He married a Swiss immigrant, Maria Jaycocks, whose name became anglicized to Mary Willcox, in the Reformed Church at Poughkeepsie, New York.[8] After many hardships as Loyalists, the Van Every family was reunited at Niagara where the sons, as members of Butler's Rangers, had their headquarters. Like some of the other soldiers' families, they camped near the fort at Niagara, cultivating a small farm. In 1782 the Van Every family was one of 16 camped near Niagara. As disbanded Loyalists the Van Every children settled at Flamboro East Township, Wentworth County, in 1783; from this point the family spread out through the rest of southern Ontario, a branch reaching Essex County by the middle of the nineteenth century. For over 100 years, one or more branches of this Loyalist family have been represented in the county of Essex.

When the Canada Southern Railway brought prosperity to Woodslee in the 1870s, a branch of the family using the spelling Vanavery set up a general store in South Woodslee. This "Great Cash Store", like other general stores in similar communities, played a social as well as a business role in the community.

Among the families which came to the area late in the century were the Van Zandts. A. B. D. Van Zandt worked as a reporter for the Windsor *Record* in the 1890s and Norman Vanzandt was a Windsor painter. Several members of the Vanzant family lived in Leamington late in the nineteenth century. They were all, despite the various spellings of the name, descendants of Adam Wenzel van Zandt, who arrived in New Amsterdam about the middle of the seventeenth century from Arnhem in the province of Gelderland.

The Van Husens were artists and photographers in Windsor late in the century, but belonged to an American branch of the Van Husen family. They did not remain in Windsor for long, but played a role in the commercial life of the area for several years.

It is difficult to distinguish between the American and Canadian branches of Loyalist families represented in the county during the last two decades of the nineteenth century. Names such as Van Luven and Van Luben mentioned in the *Illustrated Historical Atlas of Essex and Kent* (1880-1881) and various directories of this period are likely to be those of Loyalists' descendants, but could represent American families crossing and recrossing the open border.

Overall, Dutch settlement in Essex county during this time was not extensive. Although some immigrants coming directly from the Netherlands passed through Windsor in the second half of the nineteenth century, few if any remained to settle on the Canadian side of the border.

Detroit River Scene at Sunset, painted in 1891 by Frederick A. Verner. *In the centre of this watercolour is the Canadian Pacific Railway terminus, new at the time. This railway had been extended to Windsor the previous year.*

Sir William Van Horne, then president of the Canadian Pacific Railway, was trying to establish salt production on the Windsor side of the Detroit River. Organization of the Windsor Salt Company followed tests which showed that there was an excellent prospect of developing a salt industry in the area. Van Horne hoped to provide his new railway with large shipments of salt to transport to other parts of Canada.

Sir William Cornelius Van Horne (1843-1915) was president and chairman of the board of directors of the Canadian Pacific Railway from 1888 to 1910. *He was the son of Cornelius Covenhoven Van Horne, a lawyer who had moved to Illinois from New York State in the early nineteenth century, to become one of the earliest settlers of the area. The Van Horne family was descended from one of the first settlers of New Netherland, and is thought to have originally come from Hoorn in the province of North Holland in the Netherlands, although the immigrant ancestor came to America directly from Amsterdam.*

William Van Horne held various positions in American railway systems from 1857 to 1882, when he was appointed general manager of the Canadian Pacific Railway. In 1888 he became president of the railway and in 1899 he exchanged this position for that of president of the board of directors. He died in Montreal in 1915, five years after his retirement.

8

Sir William Cornelius Van Horne

In 1892 William Van Horne founded the Windsor Salt Company on Sandwich Street between Caron and Crawford Avenues, marking the beginning of an important new industry in Essex County. The founding of this company was closely tied to the development of the Canadian Pacific Railway, of which Van Horne was president.

William Cornelius Van Horne was born on 3 February 1843, the son of Mary Richards and an impoverished lawyer named Cornelius Covenhoven Van Horne. This Van Horne family was directly descended from Jan Cornelissen Van Horne of New Netherland, a close associate of the prominent Dutch West Indian Company trader Peter Minuit. Jan Cornelissen Van Horne, as one of his followers, arrived in New Netherland at the same time as Minuit in 1626. He was a citizen of Amsterdam, although it is probable that the Van Horne family originally came from Hoorn in North Holland.

Van Horne's father was born into this wealthy Dutch family of New York City early in the nineteenth century. He became a prosperous lawyer, but like so many other ambitious young men of the period, decided to go west. He left to become a homesteader at Chelsea, Illinois, a pioneer village near the departure point of the Oregon Trail. Cornelius Van Horne was a failure as a pioneer farmer and was forced to give up his homestead and move to Joliet, Illinois.

At the time of this move, William was eight years old, the eldest of five Van Horne children. In Joliet, Cornelius Van Horne opened a law practice, but not long afterwards died in an influenza epidemic, leaving his widow and five children virtually penniless. Although he left many unpaid debts, he was highly respected by the people of Illinois, in particular by the citizens of Joliet, who considered him one of the original settlers of the town. (Joliet was later to claim William Van Horne as a famous "native son", even though he had been born in Chelsea.)

As a child William Van Horne was both talented and curious. His skill as a caricaturist of schoolteachers led to his expulsion from public school after only six years of education. Undaunted, his interest in art remained strong, and as an adult he collected art seriously, owning pieces by such Dutch masters as Rembrandt and Frans Hals. His strong interest in fossils led him to become an expert palaentologist. He subsequently discovered a number of previously unknown fossils, nine of which now bear his name.

In his middle teens Van Horne decided to reach certain well-defined goals. One ambition was not to have to walk unless he chose to do so. He believed that as superintendent of a railway he would always be able to ride instead of walk. With this goal in mind he became a fully qualified telegraph operator by the age of 15, and began the steady climb to the top of his chosen career. He soon became the general manager of the St. Louis, Kansas City and Northern Railway Company. From there, in rapid succession, he held some of the best positions then available in American railroading, and by 1882 was appointed general manager of the CPR. Six years later he became its president.

The CPR arrived too late to have any effect on the settlement of Essex County, but through Van Horne's efforts the railway did have an important effect on its industry. On the Michigan side of the Detroit River, for instance, the salt industry was well established by the 1880s. It was widely known that important salt deposits were still to be found beneath Essex County. Despite this, salt was still imported in the 1880s.

Van Horne changed all that. Ever in search of cargo for empty rail cars, he brought in geologists who confirmed the rich deposit. In 1892, only two years after the completion of the CPR itself, the Windsor Salt Company began operations. Its plant was on the south side of Sandwich Street, with offices in the stone tower on the site of the CPR building.

Van Horne kept his name listed in the Windsor city directory well into the twentieth century, nearly to the time of his death in 1915. Although he visited Windsor from time to time, he travelled a great deal, and continued to make his permanent residence in Montreal where the head offices of the railway were located.

On two occasions he was asked by the prime minister, Sir John A. Macdonald, to accept a knighthood. He finally agreed, and in 1894 became the first non-British subject to be awarded the Order of St. Michael and St. George. While many honorary degrees were offered him, they were refused, for he believed that they should only be accepted for academic achievement.

In 1910, Sir William Van Horne retired from active connection with the CPR, and on 11 September 1915 he died in Montreal. Peter C. Newman has summed up the life of this great industrialist and railroad pioneer:

> To each day he gave his talents with such vigour that he made all the ingredients of his rich life flourish, while he increased the world's and his own material assets.[1]

It was Sir William Van Horne's railway that opened up western Canada, making possible the settlement of immigrants from Europe who came flooding into the country after 1892. Among these immigrants were some from the Netherlands, the first group of any size to come directly to Canada from the homeland. Their arrival marks the beginning of a new period in the history of the Dutch in Canada.

9

Dutch Immigration to Canada 1892-1913

During the long depression of the 1880s, economic conditions in Canada were discouraging. The population of the United States grew quickly; Canada's increased only slightly. In the period from 1871 to 1901, the Canadian population grew by an average of only about 60,000 per year. European immigrants frequently arrived in Canada, heard about the better standard of living to the south, and left.

At the beginning of the twentieth century this pattern changed. Economic improvement brought increased confidence in Canada's future. In 1896, Prime Minister Laurier proudly declared that "The twentieth century belongs to Canada". With the opening of virgin lands and free homesteads in the west, now made accessible by the railways running from coast to coast, the population soared. From 1901 to 1911, the prairies were settled at the rate of 200,000 to 300,000 per year.

With this flood came a few Dutch-American settlers and others directly from the Netherlands. Those who came across the border from the United States usually came with friends and relatives. They had been disappointed that most of the good land in the midwestern United States had already been claimed. Many of those who arrived directly from overseas planned to join relatives who had written to them about the opportunities offered to homesteaders in western Canada. And yet, most were scarcely aware of the existence of Canada. Canada was considered to be an inhospitable northern country, while the United States was the "land of promise".

In 1892 with the opening of the Canadian west to settlement, this picture changed and Canada became better known to Netherlanders. In the Netherlands, emigration agents began the work of attracting settlers for the Canadian west, travelling about the countryside speaking to groups of farmers, and distributing pamphlets that described the life of the homesteader in glowing terms. It was a time of poverty for many in the Netherlands and there were crowds of listeners interested in hearing the colourful speeches of the emigration agents. The industrial revolution had come rather late to the Netherlands. In the 1870s and in the years that followed many agricultural workers left the countryside to look for work in

This illustration appeared on the cover of a pamphlet issued by the government of Canada in 1884 in an attempt to attract new settlers for the Canadian west. *The original, in full colour, provided an attractive picture of life in Canada, showing a prairie homestead and stating*:

Manitoba
and the great

North west of America —
200 million acres
for colonization —
a free homestead
of 160 acres (65 bunders)
is provided for every head of family as well as every male colonist who has attained the age of 18.

the urban centres. There were few opportunities for improvement in living conditions for those workers who remained in rural areas, and emigration agents considered these most suited to undertake the hard work of the Canadian pioneer.

What the agents had said was true, but biased. They were employed by the Canadian railways to persuade as many new settlers as possible to emigrate to Canada and gave an entirely favourable picture of pioneer conditions on the prairies. The enthusiastic speeches of the agents did persuade a few to emigrate, but also caused a certain amount of criticism and distrust. One of the most active critics was J. Maurer, an agriculturist in the province of North Holland. He summed up the situation in a speech which he gave before a farmers' group in 1912:

> What in particular has given the emigration agent ... a bad reputation are three points which I shall give ... :
> 1. The emigrant is cheated by people who have monetary interest in his emigration.
> 2. The emigrant has no trustworthy knowledge of the land to which he is going, of the circumstances into which he will come; he cannot get any good information.
> 3. The immigrant, once arrived in a strange land, stands helpless in the midst of strangers, who speak a different language, have other characters — and for these reasons, after a short time, often meets his defeat.

Maurer urged the Dutch government to improve existing laws and to encourage the development of emigration societies to help prospective immigrants. In his own speeches, Maurer did his utmost to give the facts:

> Through an enormous amount of propaganda, Canada at present is best known as the country where one can get free land.... In Canada there are pieces of land measuring 64 hectares which you can obtain free of charge under the following conditions: (a) during three years the person who accepts such a piece of free land, a "homestead", must spend at least six months per year on this land in a "liveable" house; (b) within the three years, 12 acres must be ploughed and at least 8 seeded. Although this is very generous, the document, thus ownership rights, may be cancelled if these requirements are not met. It must be understood that "free land" is not land lying ready for the plough, but mostly bush, more or less heavy to work, in any case wilderness, so that these requirements that you must build a house in the first three years mean that you must work incredibly hard during the first three years to get your 12 hectares ready for cultivation. The person who has no money can only obtain it by first working for wages, and saving a small fortune, or, in harvest time, working for wages for someone else, and, in the winter, clearing his land and living his six months on it. Yet, usually people do not have any money when they accept this offer of free land; at least 2000 guilders is necessary, while an amount of 3000 guilders is necessary if one is to be able to be completely independent of others, and settle without first working for wages.[1]

Maurer published these speeches privately, and sold them at a low price. He was particularly careful to ensure that those who listened to the emigration agents had accurate information about wages:

> Full-time workers, with board and lodging, receive a monthly wage of 45 to 60 guilders in the east of Canada, 60 to 100 guilders in the west; seasonal workers, with board and a place to sleep (to be compared with our haymakers, or mowers ...) receive 3 to 5 guilders per day .... These are average wages.[2]

It was true that the emigration agents always referred to the successful cases and never spoke of those who failed, who could not stand the loneliness, or who had bad luck. The opportunity was there, however. For those who could undertake the back-breaking work, homesteading provided a chance to own land and become independent. In the Netherlands, these people had no hope of this. On the whole, however, Dutch farm workers were not eager to leave the Netherlands, where they had close ties to their friends and relatives. The great majority of those who did so, travelled to the west as Canadian authorities had planned.

In 1892 the first Dutch immigrants to come to Canada directly from overseas began to make their way into the country and by 1940 approximately 28,000 Dutch immigrants had entered Canada.[3] Before 1914, most Dutch immigrants arrived by ship in Quebec City. They were ordinarily not met at this point, but transferred directly to trains travelling west to Winnipeg. There they were officially met and taken to the Immigration Hall. From Winnipeg they were sent out to their destinations in the west. Some remained for a short time in Winnipeg where the Salvation Army was of great assistance, often helping needy immigrants find temporary jobs. Nevertheless, of the flood of immigrants who came to Canada between 1892 and 1914, the Dutch formed only a small portion, amounting to less than 1% of the total.

Still, small Dutch settlements were founded along the railway lines in both Saskatchewan and Alberta. The first of these sprang up in 1892 at Yorkton, Saskatchewan, where about ten Dutch families homesteaded for two years before seven of the families moved to Winnipeg. The latter became the first members of a Dutch community which quickly increased in size during the first years of the twentieth century. By 1913 the Winnipeg Dutch community was the largest in Canada, numbering about 100 people. Others continued westward to found villages in Alberta and Saskatchewan, with names such as Amsterdam, Edam, Cramersburg, and Zeelandia. After 1900, two agricultural colonies, Nieuw Nijver-

Dutch immigrants photographed in the new Assembly Hall of the Canadian Railways terminal in Halifax, Nova Scotia. *This photograph was probably taken between 1924 and 1928, when groups of Dutch immigrants frequently landed at Halifax on their way to the west of Canada. They usually travelled by rail directly to Winnipeg, where they were given assistance in reaching their destination.*

This photograph by W. J. Topley shows a family of Dutch immigrants immediately after their arrival at Quebec City about 1911. *Attracted by the offer of a free homestead in the west of Canada, such immigrants staunchly faced an unknown future, hopeful that good luck and hard work would lead to prosperity in the new land.*

dal and Neerlandia, were founded in Alberta; the latter has retained its Dutch character into modern times.

For some, a western colony was not the last stage of their travels. Many continued on to the lands of British Columbia and Washington state. A few quit Canada altogether, heading south to join friends or relatives who had tried to settle in Canada and failed.

Although most Dutch immigrants travelled to the west, some settled in the eastern part of Canada, in particular in southwestern Ontario. Most of these worked as farm labourers in Essex and Kent Counties, with many settling around Chatham. Two particular crops, sugar beets and tobacco, were rapidly gaining in importance, and great numbers of seasonal workers were needed for fieldwork. Although the wages paid to farm workers were not as high as in the west, the flat, rich farmlands of Essex and Kent Counties provided fine opportunities. While a few Dutch immigrants stayed, then, to settle permanently in Essex County, the number was actually very small. Immigration was still a matter of individuals and a few families. The 1901 Census shows that only 12 residents of Essex County, all living in the district of "Essex North", reported that they had been born in Holland; in the census of 1911 only seven people claimed Holland as their birthplace.

While few claimed to be of Dutch birth, many reported that they were of Dutch origin: in 1901, 69 in Essex North and 233 in Essex South, and in 1911, 77 in Essex North and 215 in Essex South. For census purposes, both in 1901 and 1911, residents were asked to state their national origin by giving that of their father. The figures showed some of Pennsylvania Dutch ancestry, descendants of Loyalists and Dutch-Americans, but very few who had come directly from the Netherlands.

Although the Canadian census of 1911 revealed only seven residents of Essex County who were of Dutch birth, this figure was quite misleading as an indication of "Dutch presence" in the area. By 1911, Dutch farm labourers had taken part for several seasons in the harvesting of the sugar-beets and tobacco grown in the county. They were part of the seasonal influx of migrant workers from Europe known as the "swallow migration".

This regular migration of field workers had begun in the spring of 1902 when the newly-founded Dominion Sugar Company of Wallaceburg brought from Belgium the VanDamme family, the first Flemings to settle in the area. The Wallaceburg company had heard of the Belgian farmers' expertise in cultivating sugar-beets, and hoped to adapt their methods to the Canadian situation. Many Flemings and their Dutch neighbours, from the part of Zeeland called Zeeuws Vlaanderen, were accustomed to migratory work. They left their homes in Belgium and Holland early in the year and went to the south of France to work in the fields. During the spring, they worked their way northwards through France, planting crops as they travelled, until summer brought the opportunity to harvest those same crops. This strenuous cycle was forced on many farm workers because of poverty. Many had large families to support on the wages that migratory labour could provide.

Not long after the VanDammes arrived in Wallaceburg, relatives and friends decided to join them. Soon an annual migration was taking place each year from Antwerp and other European ports to the ports of eastern Canada. The workers usually left about March or April and reached southwestern Ontario in time for planting. After the harvesting was completed in the fall, the migrants would return to Europe.

The Dominion Sugar Company, strongly interested in obtaining suitable workers, actively recruited these harvesters and arranged their passage to Canada. The usual pattern was for the worker to obtain a visa and then be issued a ticket for passage on a Canadian ship. The cost of his passage would be subtracted from his pay once he was employed in the fields. Workers were usually men between the ages of 18 and 40, and often single.

Sometimes after making several trips to Canada a married migrant worker would be able to save enough money to enable him to bring his family to Canada. First he would obtain steady employment and suitable housing. The latter was difficult to find, for migrant workers were often provided with shelter of the most primitive sort, frequently shacks in poor repair.

Those who came to harvest the crops of Essex County worked chiefly in the southern part of the county, in the district around Essex, Kingsville, and Leamington. Sugar-beets were grown extensively in Essex County at this time, while burley tobacco was also a major crop. The cultivation of flue-cured tobacco was then being conducted experimentally near Leamington by two American brothers from North Carolina, Colonel W. T. Gregory and Francis Gregory. From 1900 to 1913 when this work was underway, the coarser-leafed burley tobacco was still grown by Essex County tobacco farmers as it had been for the previous century.

Little is known about Dutch migrant workers who helped harvest Essex County cash crops in the early years of the century. They were largely from the mainland of Zeeland, the part known as Zeeuws Vlaanderen (not far from the port of Antwerp), and they were predominantly Roman Catholic. Many had friends and relatives living in the Flemish region of Belgium, and in ways were closer to Belgium than to the rest of the Netherlands, from which they were separated by the Scheldt River. In fact, they often travelled in the company of their Belgian friends who shared with them a common language.

In 1914 this annual "swallow migration" was interrupted by the outbreak of World War I. After the war, immigration from the Netherlands resumed once again, but assumed a different and more complex pattern.

Hendrik and Alice Knapper, pioneer members of the Christian Reformed Church in southwestern Ontario during its earliest years of development in this province.

10

Immigration Between The Wars, 1919-1939

In the Netherlands, the French system of inheritance, in force since Napoleonic times, ensured that when a father died, each of his children inherited an equal part of his property. As a result, Dutch farms were small, and even though farming was carried out more intensively than in earlier days, it was difficult for the owners to support their large families. Helping to harvest the cash crops of Essex and Kent Counties during the spring and summer seasons permitted these Dutch farmers to survive. It is possible that the dramatic increase noted in the Dutch population of Essex County as reported by the Census of 1921 was at least partially due to the presence of these seasonal harvesters;[1] that population was 292 in 1911 and an amazing 2,072 just ten years later.

Immediately after the war, economic conditions were poor in Canada. As yet, industries such as the Ford automobile plant in Windsor did not require many new workers. The need in Essex and Kent Counties, as elsewhere in Canada, was for farm labour.

Recurring seasonal unemployment soon caused earlier immigrants to write discouraging letters home. Even officially, many prospective immigrants were warned against leaving for Canada in such difficult times. The popular novel *Maria Chapdelaine* by Louis Hémon was often used to support this gloomy picture of life in Canada. Discouraged people returning to the Netherlands claimed that, for those other than well-trained agricultural workers, immigration proved to be a hateful experience; even the skilled had to quickly adapt to farming methods unfamiliar to them in the Netherlands.

In spite of all the gloomy warnings the Dutch began to look with more favour on the idea of Canada in the early 1920s. Books and articles recommending "careful" immigration began to change public opinion. It was suggested that farmers and farm workers should send for their families only after they had become well established. These writers recommended eastern rather than western Canada, although the official government policy encouraged movement to the unpopulated prairies.

Directed immigration by the Canadian government had hardly existed before World War I. Before the mid-1890s it had been unregulated, and even after this time there were few government regulations to impede the flow of the large number of immigrants needed to populate the Canadian west.

After World War I, economic considerations and religious and racial difference came to the fore. The immigration Act was created in an effort to secure the population already in Canada from possible competition. Certain undesirables such as criminals and spies, were not permitted entry. For others, permission to settle in Canada was considered a privilege rather than a right.

Dutch and Belgians were preferred immigrants and had little difficulty being allowed into Canada to work or to live permanently. After 1922 they no longer needed visas to enter Canada. At Rotterdam and Antwerp, Canadian government agents distributed attractive booklets informing passersby of the rich opportunities awaiting. Ten thousand copies of one of these promotional pamphlets were published in the Dutch language in the 1920s, for distribution in Flanders and the Netherlands.

Before 1924, more Belgians than Dutch entered Canada as immigrants. In that year, however, this changed, as the American authorities began to enforce their stringent immigration regulations for the first time. In 1921, they had set up an official quota system. Accordingly, the United States was willing to accept, each year, only an additional 3% of the number of people of that ethnic group residing in America as of the census of 1910. That final 3% figure was 3,607. In 1924, the quota was changed to represent 2% of the population according to the 1890 census, which meant a lowering of the number of Dutch admitted to 2,003.

The effect of this quota system was immediate. Some of the Dutch who had relatives or friends in Western Michigan, had to settle near the border and wait for a chance to enter the United States. This "temporary immigration" was, of course, strongly discouraged by the Canadian immigration authorities, who were looking for those who would take up permanent residence in Canada.

In 1924 there was a definite increase in the number of Dutch immigrants to Canada. Some were migrant workers who had saved enough to rent or buy a small farm of their own. Others were young farmers or farm labourers who were without job prospects in the Netherlands. Some were simply adventurers and wanted to seek their fortune in a foreign country. They all hoped to gain economic stability in Canada where the prospects seemed better than at home.

At this time, emigration societies in the Netherlands began to play a larger role in providing information and assistance to those who were planning to emigrate. The first of these societies, the Christian Emigration Society, had been founded as early as 1892. A second society, of a semi-official nature, was the Netherlands Emigration League, already referred to, founded in 1913 through the efforts of interested organizations and some dedicated individuals such as J. Maurer. The work of this society was interrupted by World War I, but after the War was over, its efforts recommenced. In 1918 the Netherlands Migration Society was founded, followed by the Central Emigration Foundation Holland in 1923. The Roman Catholic Emigration Society began operations in 1925 and the Roman Catholic Emigration Congress in 1927. The Calvinistic Christian Emigration Society was founded in 1925 and the Calvinist Emigration Society in 1927.[2]

One of the chief aims of all these emigration societies was to provide facts to counter the propaganda aimed at the Dutch. They stressed the need for accurate information before setting out for Canada and outlined the necessary preparations which should be made by prospective immigrants. They printed letters from immigrants, including vivid descriptions of the loneliness faced by newcomers in a community, particularly in a land with great geographical distances and a small population. The Roman Catholic Emigration Congress and the Calvinistic Christian Emigration Society had additional goals as well. These organizations believed that those who left the Netherlands had an obligation to fulfill as immigrants in a new land. Not only must they retain their faith by settling near others who share their religious beliefs, but they were duty-bound to act as missionaries in the country of their destination. At this time, the Canadian government was against the idea of group settlements and would not issue free land to homesteaders who wanted to settle in religious groups; immigrants to Canada had to go as individuals.[3] The religious societies were therefore much concerned with preparing immigrants, fearing that their members would eventually lose contact with others who shared their religion.

The emigration societies of the Netherlands were greatly relieved when the Canadian government stopped using agents of the Canadian railways to offer land to immigrants. After 1917 their function was carried out by the Land Settlement Board, which gave valuable assistance to immigrants who needed employment and a place to live. The Canadian railways did, however, continue to influence the Canadian government by encouraging immigration and influencing the placement of immigrants.

While emigration societies, agents, and government bodies aided many of the Dutch who settled in Canada, others came quite independently. They usually followed friends or relatives who had gone to Canada earlier and were prepared to help in making the adjustment to life in the new country.

It is difficult to know how many Dutch immigrants settled in Essex County in the period between the two world wars. Canadian government statistics show how many intended to settle in the province of Ontario, but not the number who moved on to live in other provinces, or returned to the Netherlands. There were many Dutch who lived and worked in Essex County for some years in the 1920s but left the area and were not present to be included in the census of 1931. Many Dutch and Belgians, particularly from the Leamington area, left in 1928 and 1929 when flue-cured tobacco became a successful cash crop around Delhi and Tillsonburg.

Many Dutch names are on file in the lists of field workers kept by the Tobacco Marketing Board after 1924. Lists of workers and their nationalities were also kept by the Dominion Sugar Company in Wallaceburg.

The Catholic Dutch continued to be closely associated with the Belgians and joined in their recreational activities. These included amateur theatricals arranged by a cultural group known as Vlaanderen's Kerels. This patriotic society founded in 1927 continued an old custom familiar to the immigrants in their home villages in Flanders — the presentation of plays for both instruction and entertainment. The repertoire included both modern and classical plays, including those of Vondel, all performed in the Dutch language. They were enjoyed by large crowds of immigrants in Chatham and Windsor. There were also religious processions at St. Mary's Church in Blenheim, where the Capuchins opened a monastery in 1927. A banner in honour of Our Lady of Flanders, brought from Belgium, was carried at the head of the religious processions which were conducted in the manner familiar to the immigrants.

The opening of the church at Blenheim, in fact, was the direct result of Dutch and Flemish movement to the area around Chatham and the southern part of Essex County between 1924 and 1927. Some of the newcomers came from North Holland, the most over populated part of the Netherlands, while others came from the province of Groningen. However, the majority were from Limburg, North Brabant, and Zeeland. They were predominantly Roman Catholic, and by moving into Kent and Essex Counties, came under the Diocese of London.

The arrival of thousands of Dutch-speaking Catholics in a diocese where not a single priest had a command of Dutch created the type of situation feared most by the Catholic emigration organizations of the Netherlands. A Dutch Roman Catholic, in order to fulfill his religious obligations, had need of a Dutch-speaking priest.

One of the most concerned observers of this situation was a missionary priest, Father Theophilus van den Heufel, a member of the Dutch province of the Capuchin order. He had accompanied a large group of Dutch immigrants from the Netherlands to southwestern Ontario. He expressed his concern to the bishop of the diocese, the Most Reverend M. F. Fallon, of London. Bishop Fallon wrote to the Father General of the Capuchin Order in Rome asking for assistance with this problem, made more acute each spring by the arrival of new immigrants from Belgium and the Netherlands. On 21 March 1927 a proposal was made by the general of the Capuchin order in a letter written to the Belgian province of the order by Father Fredegand of Rome:

> ... In view of his own obligation to care for their spiritual welfare, the Bishop has asked Father General to accept a settlement in his diocese, with priests who can serve them in their own language. He offers Blenheim, where there is a small church, no rectory as yet, but would seem to offer fair prospects for future development.
>
> Father General would like to know if the Belgian Province would have four priests available to serve these people in Flemish in Ontario, which is, as you know, one of the most prosperous provinces in Canada. These four priests would not have to leave as a group; two could start, and two more could be added later.[4]

This proposal was accepted by the Belgian province of the order, and on 29 August 1927, Father Willibrord of Mortsel, Belgium, and Father Ladislas of Zondereigen, Belgium, left Antwerp by ship. They were welcomed at the Chatham railway station on September 14 by Father R. H. Dignan, pastor of Blessed Sacrament Church in Chatham. That same day, Father Dignan drove them by car to Blenheim to see the small church and the unfinished rectory where they were soon to live. They remained with Father Dignan for three more days before moving into their quarters. Throughout the years, Father Dignan remained their friend and benefactor.

Some weeks later, two other Capuchins, Father Polycarp and Brother Mansuetus, were assigned to join Father Willibrord and Father Ladislas. They left Antwerp on 2 November 1927 and arrived in Blenheim on November 14. In April 1928, still another Capuchin priest, Father Damasus of Bruges, left Antwerp to join the mission.

This small group of Capuchins, their numbers reinforced from time to time by other members of the order from Belgium, were to have a profound influence on Dutch-speaking Catholics in the counties of Essex and Kent during the following 50 years.

While the majority of Dutch immigrants to southwestern Ontario in the 1920s were Roman Catholics, there were a considerable number of Calvinists as well.[6] Those liberal Calvinists who belonged to the Reformed Church in the Netherlands (*Hervormd*) often became associated with one of the large Canadian Protestant denominations, usually the Presbyterian Church, or after 1925, the United Church of Canada.

There were particularly close ties between the members of the Christian Reformed Church, founded by a group of strictly orthodox Seceders in Grand Rapids, Michigan in 1857, and the orthodox *Gereformeerde* churches of the Netherlands. The Dutch language was still spoken in many Christian Reformed homes in Michigan and the clergy were able to give assistance to Dutch newcomers in their own language. When there was a prospect of many of their members immigrating to Canada, with a possible loss of contact with others who shared their faith, orthodox Calvinists in the Netherlands took up contact with the ministry of the Christian Reformed Church in Grand Rapids. The home missionaries of the Christian Reformed Church had been active in Canada earlier in the century, having established churches in western Canada. In 1925 the home missionary work of this church was resumed in southern Ontario, including Kent and Essex Counties.

A report on missionary work in Ontario appeared in the Christian Reformed Church Yearbook for 1926, where it was reported that three missions had already been opened:

> The greater proportion of our people live in the southern part of the province, and we have already opened mission stations in Toronto, Chatham, and Windsor .... We have just begun work in Canada, and have still a great deal to learn about this great and wealthy country, but there is no doubt that the Lord has provided, for our people and for our church, an open door to welcome us into Canada. The overpopulated Netherlands have need of underpopulated Canada, and the Canadians, as was repeatedly made clear to us, are very happy to have gained our Dutch people [for their own country].[5]

The missionary went on to report that at the time of writing, (January 1926), there was a high rate of unemployment in Toronto, but that in the summer months there were many opportunities for employment on the farms of southwestern Ontario. The annual report on mission work in Canada ended with the names of the *scriba* for each of the three mission churches. The *scriba* for the Windsor mission was B. Van Lith, 125 Tournier Street, Sandwich, Ontario.

The report for the following year, published in the Christian Reformed Yearbook for 1927, showed that the Chatham mission church, in the heart of the beet-sugar and tobacco district, was already the largest and most active of the three missions. Dr. Brink, the missionary for the area, reported on the founding of the congregation:

> To understand the intense joy that fills such hearts one must, onself, have lived several months without Word and Sacraments in the language we can understand.
>
> We hope that this young congregation will continue to grow, and that they will have joy in their growth.[6]

Among the members of this congregation was Hendrik Knapper, a 23-year-old immigrant from Groningen, who was working on a farm in Blackwell, near Sarnia. He was living with his wife Alice and two small children when he was visited by the Reverend J. Brink. This missionary was travelling in southwestern Ontario searching for orthodox Calvinist families among the many Dutch immigrants working as farm labourers in the area. When he located a few, he formed groups and preached to them in their homes. At the time he visited the Knapper family, there were only two other Dutch Calvinist families in the Blackwell area.

Later, the Knapper family was visited by the Rev. Simon Dijkstra, a missionary who had been forced to leave China by its war with Japan. He was assigned to serve the Lee Street Christian Reformed Church in Chatham and also preached to families on farms in the area. It was he who suggested to Hendrik Knapper that he might wish to move to Windsor where the Ford Motor Company was looking for labourers. Hendrik Knapper was hired by Ford at fifty cents an hour, considered a good rate of pay at that time.

The Knapper family joined the Windsor Christian Reformed congregation in 1928. At first, the congregation met at St. Andrew's Presbyterian Church with Rev. W. Meyer of Grand Rapids as its minister. Later, it moved to the headquarters of the Young Men's and Women's Christian Association in Windsor. As unemployment grew in the depression years, the congregation dwindled until only the Knappers remained.

During the worst of the depression years from 1929 to 1935, Windsor had an unusually high rate of unemployment due to its dependence on the badly-affected automotive industry. Some of the Dutch, (mostly Christian Reformed), left Windsor and went to Holland Marsh, where a Dutchman, John Snor, carried out a remarkable reclamation project in the marshlands to the north of Toronto. This project was intended to help unemployed Dutch immigrants by giving them the opportunity to farm for themselves on reclaimed land. Conditions in Holland Marsh were extremely difficult for the settlers there, but through perseverence they established a successful colony in what has become one of the most productive farming areas of Ontario.

In 1931 the Canadian Census was taken again with clear instructions to the enumerator, which read:

> ORIGIN IS TO BE TRACED THROUGH THE FATHER!
> A person whose father is English and whose mother is French will be recorded as of English origin.

The population in Essex County of those having Dutch origin was reported as 2,241.

Many of those who claimed to be of Dutch origin were of course Dutch-American, Pennsylvania Dutch, United Empire Loyalist, or Mennonite. Mennonites had arrived in number in Essex County in 1924, coming from Russia. The origin of some could be traced to the Netherlands from where a few of their ancestors had migrated centuries earlier.

During the Depression years, immigration from the Netherlands to Canada dwindled. Economic conditions were poor in both countries, and thus there was little incentive to immigrate to Canada. Stringent regulations were enforced by the Canadian authorities to keep immigrants from entering Canada if they were to provide competition for Canadian workers. While World War II raged, immigration to Canada from the Netherlands came to a halt. Some Dutch-Americans continued to enter the country, but not in any appreciable number.

During the war a number of Dutch "war volunteers" came to Canada for military training. Other volunteers were in training in England where the Dutch armed forces had assembled after the invasion of the Netherlands in the spring of 1940. Tony Koning, from Heiloo in North Holland, was in the Dutch armed forces at the time of its retreat through the Netherlands, Belgium, and France, to England. In 1941 he volunteered to go with other Dutch administrators from England to Canada to assist in the training programme. In 1943, he returned to England when the camp in Stratford was closed, for it was evident that all Dutchmen who had managed to escape to Canada had been given an opportunity for training. The Dutch war volunteers followed the Canadian forces into the battle for the liberation of the Netherlands. In this way, they returned to their homeland near the conclusion of the war, arriving in late 1944 and early 1945. Koning was one of the war volunteers who later decided to make Canada his home.

William Reybroek keeps 80 pigeons and races them from May to October. *The pigeons are trained while young, banded, and released in races, during which they fly from 100 to 700 kilometres in order to return home.*

At the age of 19, Reybroek immigrated to Canada from Boekel, a town in North Brabant province in the Netherlands, where he had trained as a carpenter. From 1935 to 1953 he worked for the Ford Motor Company of Canada. After 18 years there, he decided to leave and set up his own carpentry business. Although now retired, he still enjoys woodworking. He first returned to the Netherlands in 1968 after 43 years in Canada. Since then he has returned six times to visit friends and relatives.

A formal picture of the bridal party, taken at the wedding reception of Helena van Adel and Hervé Gravel in November 1945, in s'Hertogenbosch. *The bride was a telephone operator, and the groom a member of the 23rd. Canadian Engineers.*

Helena van Adel's mother's family was originally from Zeeland, her father's family from Tiel. Hervé Gravel's childhood home was in East Broughton in Quebec, near the area where his immigrant ancestor from Normandy had settled in the seventeenth century.

In November 1946, Helena Gravel travelled with her two-month-old daughter Johanna to the Kurhaus in Scheveningen, the Netherlands, to join other "war-brides" and children en route to Canada. The Dutch group went by boat to the Hook of Holland, where they boarded the "bride ship" Empire Brent, bound first for Liverpool. After joining a similar contingent of British war-brides in London and returning by train to Liverpool, the entire group, numbering 900 women and children, left aboard the Empire Brent for Canada. Despite a collision with a cattle boat that forced the ship to return for repairs, the Empire Brent finally landed in Halifax. Boarding one of the special "bride trains" provided to move these newcomers to their destinations across Canada, Helena and Johanna Gravel arrived in Windsor five days before the Christmas of 1946.

Johanna later married Frank Foster, the son of a Scottish war-bride and her Polish husband who had served in a Polish unit of the British army. Johanna Foster has maintained both her Dutch language, and regular contact with her Dutch relatives, most of whom are in the area of Sliedrecht. She is treasurer of CAANS and active in its local Windsor chapter, and is currently head of Collection Development at the Leddy Library of the University of Windsor.

11

Post-War Immigration 1946-1960

The majority of Dutch immigrants to Canada, and to Essex County, came during the years directly following World War II. The first of this group to arrive, in 1946, were the Dutch war-brides and their children. A record of these, made on 31 December 1946, showed that 1,886 Dutch wives and 428 children were dependants of Canadian servicemen. Several of these war-brides came to Essex County, while the others scattered across Canada. They usually joined their husbands' relatives until they could find a home of their own in an area where their husbands had found work.

As well as war-brides, there were "war-grooms".[1] Tony Koning was one of those. He had met his wife Jean in Stratford when he served there as a war volunteer. While he first worked as an accountant, he was later ordained as an Anglican priest, and in that capacity came to Essex County.

An additional category of these Dutch immigrants consisted of those people suffering the immediate effects of the war. Betsy Cohen of Amsterdam was one of these. She had spent most of the war years in hiding. Later she moved to the United States, in a special programme for Jewish emigrants from the Netherlands. After living there for nearly 20 years, and training as a social worker, she moved with her husband to Essex County.

In 1947, large-scale immigration to Canada began. It was to continue for more than a decade before there was a gradual decrease in the annual number of Dutch immigrants. During those years, there were complex and unusual circumstances both in Canada and the Netherlands which led many Netherlanders to uproot themselves from their homes and establish new ones in Canada.

Surveys made in the years 1946-1952 show how many of the Dutch were in favour of emigration at the time. Each year, a cross-section of the population was asked the question: "If you had a choice, would you prefer to stay in the Netherlands or would you rather go and live in another country?" The answers appear below.

The circumstances which led so many to think seriously about the advantages of emigration were in part the result of World War II, which caused devastation throughout the Netherlands. When the Germans

	NIPO surveys[2]			Emigration	
	In favour of remaining in the Netherlands %	In favour of emigration %	No opinion %	Number of emigrants (thousands)	Per 10,000 inhabitants
1946	75	22	3	0.5	1
1947	60	32	8	6.8	8
1948	56.5	32.5	11	13.8	16
1949	67	29	4	13.9	16
1950	70	25	5	21.3	21
1951	69	26	5	37.6	36
1952	76	21	3	48.6	46[2]

left the country, it had been stripped of all moveable property, including entire industrial plants which had been systematically sent to Germany during the war years. Approximately four percent of the homes had been destroyed, nearly a tenth of the agricultural land flooded. Until the salt could be removed from the soil, normal crops could not be grown successfully. The devastated economy needed to be improved by a series of emergency measures:

> Priority number one was to import fuel and food for the famished population and to get production going. Potatoes, the staple diet of the Dutch, were rationed for a year and a half, bread for three and a half years; the last of the consumer goods to be derationed was coffee, which did not become available on the free market until 1952. Similarly, the whole community was organized to fight tuberculosis, the incidence of which had increased greatly during the occupation.[3]

The Dutch people had suffered a series of crises beginning with the economic depression of the early 1930s, continuing with the German invasion in 1940, and the years of occupation, 1940-1945. These shocks had caused a change in attitude toward emigration which became apparent after the war. People whose lives had already been seriously disrupted were not as hesitant to face the difficulties of adjustment in a foreign country.

Fear of a new war which grew in the early post-war years was also a factor in the emigration decisions of some of the Dutch, especially in 1948. In 1949 this fear decreased somewhat when the Netherlands and Indonesia signed an agreement marking the end of hostilities there. The lifting of the blockade of Berlin in 1949 helped make the Dutch more optimistic about the possibility of continued peace in Europe.

There was a serious housing shortage in the Netherlands after the war. For many years, some married couples had to live with relatives or share accomodation with strangers. Young people often had to postpone marriage because of a lack of suitable housing. There was a strong awareness of the overpopulation of the country, which led to great concern about the prospect of future unemployment.

The loss of the Dutch East Indies in 1949 also had a disastrous effect on the economy of the Netherlands. The subsequent return of many Dutch people from the Indies added to the population burden. Many of the newcomers, accustomed to a freer life in the tropics, were unable to make an easy adjustment to the confined and rather grim conditions which prevailed in the Netherlands after the war. Many of them, uprooted once by the war in the Indies, decided to emigrate again. Several of these families eventually settled in Essex County.[4]

The Dutch authorities attempted to solve the many problems of this post-war period by implementing three large-scale plans. One of these was to promote industrialization. It was thought that this would lead to more opportunities for employment and increased international trade. It was also hoped that industrialization would cause a decrease in the high birth rate, since rural families tended to have larger families than urban ones. Birth control measures were not considered because of the opposition of most church members, in particular Roman Catholics and orthodox Calvinists. Many of the religious leaders of these churches wished to have the new industries situated away from the large population centres hoping that the workers would be able to retain their rural values. One of the reasons why many Calvinists left the Netherlands was to avoid the industrialization process which, indeed, within a few years was to lead to the development of Randstad, a large urban area covering much of the western portion of the country in the area of Amsterdam, Utrecht, Haarlem, The Hague, and Rotterdam.

Another plan was to carry out a huge reclamation project in the IJselmeer. The Dutch government hoped that the newly-reclaimed land would provide farms for the children of large farm families. However, it was soon apparent that the land could not be reclaimed quickly enough to keep pace with the great increase in manpower available. There remained a large surplus of farm workers and a shortage of farmland.

A third idea, to sponsor emigration, soon gained support. Until 1947, only landless farm workers were encouraged to leave. Within a few years, however, the Dutch government was encouraging the departure of all who were capable of emigrating.

Canada was the first country with which the Netherlands negotiated an immigration agreement. Following six months of negotiations, the first Dutch farm settlers began arriving in June 1947, under the scheme known as the "Netherland Farm Families Movement". First, single farm workers were allowed into Canada. Then, progressively larger groups were brought in, according to a plan set up carefully by the two governments.

In Windsor, eight new immigration officers were hired to deal with the large number of immigrants expected to settle in the border area.

The question of housing was a pressing one. During the war years, both men and women from rural districts had come into industrial centres such as Windsor to work in the factories. Some farms were abandoned and the countryside was no longer heavily populated, particularly in the south of Essex County. In preparation for the new immigrants of 1947, Rev. Mark Nelissen, a Belgian Capuchin priest in Blenheim, made a survey of the farms in southern Kent and Essex Counties. He counted the farm homes which were available to newcomers, and reported to the immigration authorities so that arrangements could be made to bring a suitable number of Roman Catholic farm families from the Netherlands and Belgium into the area. Most of these Dutch Catholic families, from the provinces of North Brabant and Limburg, were given the same practical and spiritual assistance by the priests at Blenheim as the Dutch and Belgian Catholics who arrived before World War II.

There was a strongly favourable attitude towards immigration in the rural areas of Kent and Essex Counties. As soon as the war was over, various public and private organizations approached the federal government in Ottawa to urge that immigrants be brought into Canada to fill the need for labour, especially farm labour. One of the most vocal of these pressure groups was the Canadian and Dominion Sugar Refining Company of Chatham. This company asked particularly for Dutch workers, who enjoyed a fine reputation for their industriousness. To be assured of workers, the company sponsored immigrants, guaranteeing that those it sponsored would have at least six months of work, and would not become a public expense during that time. Living

John Fase, general manager at the Winco Engineering Company in Windsor in 1959, four years after he immigrated from the Netherlands. *He was born in Gouda, and was living in Boskoop prior to leaving the Netherlands in July 1955. In Boskoop he was manager of a television repair service. Nearly 30 years later he still works in the same field, now managing his own repair business in Windsor, where he remanufactures television picture tubes.*

quarters were supplied until these immigrant families became established, often free of charge. Immigrants who came to southwestern Ontario under this plan were in an advantageous position, for they could soon move on to find other work if they wished. Eventually, most of the Dutch sugar company workers were able to settle on farms of their own. This caused a large turnover of workers, and for nearly two decades after the war, the company continued to sponsor immigration to the sugar-beet areas of Kent and Essex County.

Among the other organizations which sponsored immigration to the area was the Christian Reformed Church, which had sent missionaries in before World War II. There was renewed contact between the headquarters of the church in Grand Rapids, Michigan, and church leaders of the *Gereformeerde* churches in the Netherlands:

> In the winter of 1946 representatives of the church in Southwestern Ontario held a meeting in Woodstock to make preparations for an envisaged large-scale migration of Dutch and a committee was organized to take this migration under study. In March of the following year a second meeting was held whereby the missionary-at-large from the church at Grand Rapids was also present. This meeting had as a result that a sum of money was granted to the committee by the Grand Rapids administration to assist the incoming settlers and to promote further immigration to the region.[5]

Those first Calvinists of 1947 were members of the strictly orthodox *Gereformeerde Kerken, Onderhoudende Art. 31*. They were met and received into the home of the Knappers, by then the sole remaining members of the Christian Reformed Church founded in Windsor in 1925. As more potential Christian Reformed Church members arrived, Hendrik Knapper asked the Grand Rapids chapter for assistance. Soon, two Christian Reformed fieldmen were assigned to meet the incoming Calvinists at their port of arrival (usually by train from Quebec), and escorting them on the train journey to their destination. John Vellinga of Chatham, a Dutch businessman who had immigrated to Canada before World War II, was the fieldman instrumental in assisting many orthodox Calvinist immigrants to settle in the area around Essex. He accompanied newcomers to Chatham where he lived. Vellinga then returned home, and these immigrants continued by train to Windsor where John Napier, an immigration officer, was expecting them. He would arrange that Hendrik Knapper, or, in later years, Ben Lever, would meet the train and welcome them. These immigrants would be given temporary shelter in the Knapper home or housed in tourist cabins by the Department of Immigration, then driven to the farms where their sponsors were awaiting them.

In the southern part of Essex County, members of the *Netherlands Hervormde*[6] church were assisted by the Rutgers and Vriezen families who were helpful to immigrants who were liberal Calvinists.

The first large groups of Dutch immigrants arrived in Chatham in June 1947. Most of these 250 newcomers settled near there, though a few continued on to Essex County. It was only somewhat later, when many had settled around Chatham, that a significant number moved to the area around Essex. Others went to farms around Kingsville and Leamington. Some of the Dutch women found seasonal work in the Heinz cannery in Leamington which provided additional income for the family.

Most of the immigrant heads of families were in their thirties or forties at their time of arrival. Families often had ten or twelve children. They were not allowed to leave the Netherlands until a sponsor had been arranged for them. This was a duty of the fieldman who would find a suitable sponsor who agreed to provide employment and housing.

The situation of the sponsored immigrant has been described as follows:

> In case the immigrant was sponsored by a Canadian farmer, he worked full time for his new boss while other members of the family either assisted on the farm or went to work in the cash crops or industries in town. Starting wages were often less than had been expected and especially the family with few children had a tough row to hoe. Add to this the unfamiliarity with farm equipment, different farm practices, strange surroundings, and language problems, and it can easily be imagined that many families had the urge of returning to their homeland.
>
> By the same token, living accommodations, although provided for by the sponsor, were generally not what the family had been used to either from the point of space or facilities, and for the immigrant wife especially the first months in the new abode were generally difficult to say the least. But although some faltered when faced with the multitude of problems they encountered, most of these women accepted the challenge, knowing that eventually they would be able to move into a home of their own.
>
> Despite the handicaps laid in the path of the immigrants it is remarkable to note the great strides made by many of them after having been in the region a comparatively short time. Through thrift and the pooling of the wages earned during long hours of work, numerous families were in a position to purchase their own property after only three years or less.[7]

Thus, one of the greatest areas of concentration of Dutch immigration was in southwestern Ontario. While Essex County received a fairly large number of the immigrants, Kent, Lambton, Middlesex, and Elgin Counties received considerably more. Chatham, as it had been from the early 1920s onward, remained the centre of Dutch settlement.

Helga Harder, programme director of Iona College, a college maintained by the United Church of Canada, and affiliated with the University of Windsor. *This photograph was taken in the winter of 1983, shortly after her return from four years in Japan, where she and her husband taught at the International Christian University in Tokyo. Here she is seen consulting her family history, which traces her European origins over a 200-year period.*

Harder has Dutch Mennonites on both sides of her family. They were descendants of Mennonites from Danzig, Prussia, brought to Russia by Catherine The Great of Russia during the eighteenth century. When the Trans-Siberian Railway was partly built, the Russian government offered free land to settlers. Among those pioneers were Mennonites from the Ukraine, including Helga Harder's ancestors. Helga Harder's parents met in Kitchener, as newly arrived immigrants from Russia.

Map of modern Essex County.

12

Development of a Dutch Community

Beginning in 1950, immigrants from the Netherlands included not only farmers, but people with business, professional, and technical backgrounds. Most of these newcomers came from urban areas of the Netherlands and chose to live in cities and towns in Canada. While the majority of those who came to Ontario found work in Toronto or vicinity, some did travel on to southwestern Ontario. Often, as in previous years, the newcomers chose Essex County because friends or relatives had come to the area earlier. The city of Windsor's location on the international border continued to attract immigrants who hoped to leave for the United States when the opportunity arose. Still others were attracted by the high wages offered by Windsor industries, in particular the automobile factories. In the late 1940s and early 1950s immigrants of many nationalities streamed into Windsor, where most of them found accommodation in the central part of the city. There were relatively few Dutch among them since most of the immigrants from the Netherlands continued to pass through Windsor en route to rural destinations.

The Windsor community took steps to help all these "New Canadians" adjust to life in Canada. Foremost among those who offered counselling and practical assistance to immigrants of all nationalities was Lena Farell, the director of the Young Men and Young Women's Christian Association of Windsor. As soon as the influx of immigrants began in 1947 she established a series of programmes especially designed for immigrants. These included free language instruction in classes which met one evening per week in the Y.M.C.A. headquarters in downtown Windsor. Volunteer instructors, few of whom were professional teachers, joined immigrants in an informal classroom setting to help with conversational English. Often, 50 or more took part in this programme (which is still offered today). As well as classes in English, the New Canadians were given opportunities to attend such entertainments as picnics and barbecues, some planned just for them. Some of these Y.M.C.A. volunteers were members of women's social societies. Prominent among such organizations was the Imperial Order of the Daughters of the Empire, which held dances and parties for the New Canadians, supplying the entertainment and refreshments as a gesture of goodwill.

As immigrants of many nationalities looking for jobs in industry poured into Windsor, community efforts to receive them multiplied. The Board of Education of the City of Windsor established classes in Canadian citizenship and various levels of instruction in "English for New Canadians". In 1951, Willistead Library, a large mansion which had been given to the City of Windsor, became one of the centres of this activity:

> The literature class is one of a number of activities which enliven Willistead Library every Tuesday evening. In one room lessons are given in Basic English, and in another, "English for engineers." In a third there is a record player and a set of Linguaphone American English records. There are classes in Canadian geography and history in the Film Room. An old-fashioned spelling bee, a film show, a discussion of Canadian manners and customs, or a trip to a local automobile factory may be the special feature of the evening. In any case, enough activities are planned, or develop spontaneously during the evening, that each of the New Canadians, whatever his ability in English, has a chance to spend two or three hours practising his new language.

These classes were started in July 1951, in answer to a growing need for some practical method of helping the individual New Canadian with his particular language difficulties. Almost every day there would be a New Canadian in the library asking for help in filling out a government form, or in writing a business letter. Others wanted help in finding a teacher to give private instruction in English, since the regular Board of Education night school classes in English for New Canadians had closed for the term. As the need seemed so urgent, it was decided to organize small, informal classes to meet the emergency. Any New Canadian who came to the library for assistance was invited to come to "conversational English" classes, to be held each Tuesday evening during the summer. The local Red Cross Corps cooperated with the library in this project by providing volunteer teachers to assist the librarians, and by permitting the group to use the Corp's rooms as a meeting place during the summer months. In the fall the classes moved to Willistead Library, and have since been held there under the sponsorship of the Windsor Public Library Board. The cataloguing room, Art Gallery, Film Room, and nooks and crannies not otherwise in use have been pressed into service as classrooms.

The classes grew in size until there was an average attendance of fifty. Soon the problem of finding a sufficient number of volunteer teachers became acute. A number of additional volunteers, school teachers and members of the I.O.D.E., were obtained through the cooperation of the Citizenship Association of Windsor. Then the Windsor Council on Group Relations sent its members to lend their assistance. By February, when a timely newspaper article drew attention to the project and brought many offers of assistance, the volunteer teachers included librarians, high school students, social workers, engineers, teachers, and interested citizens of Windsor, all drawn together by a common interest in New Canadians and their problems, and a desire to help them. Since the beginning of the project over one hundred English-speaking people have given their assistance in some way.[1]

Soon, social workers, teachers, religious organizations, and members of the community at large were assisting the newcomers, particularly those who could not yet understand English. A concerted effort was made to come to their aid with a new organization, the Citizenship Association of Windsor. Its founder was Edith Ferguson, a Canadian social worker who had returned to Canada from Europe where she had aided refugees in the camps for displaced persons maintained by the United Nations. The separate Citizenship Council of Windsor, which was composed of representatives of the various groups concerned with immigrants, gave advice and practical help to its member organizations.

This assistance was necessitated by the many problems that arose, as thousands of New Canadians passed through or settled in the city. A worker at the Catholic Immigration Centre in Windsor described the situation as follows:

> In the first few weeks, having collected sufficient furniture, bedding, stoves, washing machines, pots and pans,ced cutlery and other furnishings, we thought that from then on, all we had to do, was to give our New Canadians temporary housing and as soon as the bread-winner of the family obtained a job, help them to find a house and then they would be safely installed in a Parish area and that would be another family of New Canadians well on their way to becoming excellent citizens in our community.
>
> Instead of the end of our efforts, this was just the beginning. Our first rude awakening was the exploitation of New Canadians. This is possibly one of the most disgraceful conditions in the ranks of labour. These are some of the conditions which we rectified locally. A former European man advertised for domestic work in the local papers. He would fill the jobs with New Canadians, collect the going wage from the employer, and then pay the employees a paltry 25 cents an hour. A field manager for a canning factory, moving New Canadian families out to farms for the harvesting of crops and setting them up in buildings that a farmer would not use for his cattle or chickens. A bowling alley using New Canadians to set up pins, and a car washer employing New Canadians on the wash line, and in both cases paying wages far *below* the normal or going wage. Possibly the

68

Dutch and Italian immigrants in 1952, soon after their arrival from Europe. *The men are from Italy, the women from the Netherlands. They are seen studying Basic English with the assistance of Joan Magee, organizer of the classes held at Willistead Public Library. By 1952 such classes had been held for three years on Tuesday evenings throughout the entire year. This permitted students to join these informal groups as the need and opportunity arose. Basic English readers and workbooks geared to four levels of difficulty were provided free of charge by the Ontario government. There was no charge for tuition since the classes were taught by volunteers from the community, including librarians, professional teachers, social workers, engineers, Red Cross volunteers, members of the Imperial Order of the Daughters of the Empire, and homemakers. Attendance at each of these weekly classes ranged from 50 to 200 students, and over 1,000 New Canadians received assistance with their English studies in this way between 1950 and 1957.*

In January 1983, Sylvia Thijs became the first formal classroom instructor of the Dutch language in Windsor. *The introductory class in conversational Dutch was initiated as a non-credit "general interest" course by the Windsor Board of Education due to popular demand for the subject. Over 20 adult students attended this ten-week evening course. Most students planned to further their knowledge of Dutch after this beginner's course.*

Dutch-language books from the Windsor Public Library collection served as a useful resource for these students. Books from the Dutch-language collection at the National Library of Canada and from the Southwestern Regional Library System were added to increase the list of current and large-print publications.

Sylvia Thijs is an elementary school teacher in Windsor. She taught in her native Friesland in the Netherlands, and in Indonesia before coming to Canada. Thijs obtained her Ontario teacher's certificate and Bachelor of Arts degree fromb the University of Windsor. She is active in the Windsor Chapter of CAANS, *and in 1982 carried out extensive interviews of Dutch-speaking residents of Essex County in preparation for this book.*

This picture of Evert Van Doorn appeared first in *The Windsor Star*, August 1982, and later in the Toronto *Globe and Mail*. It was published with the caption: "Ev Van Doorn, a contractor in Windsor, Ontario, carries on an age-old Dutch tradition [of] wearing clogs. He has safely dropped bricks and concrete blocks on them". These shoes, called klompen by the Dutch, are worn chiefly in the moist lowlands of the Netherlands, particularly by farmers, gardeners, and construction workers. They are readily available for purchase at plant nurseries in Essex County, and at the annual Dutch Market sponsored by the Neerlandia Society of Windsor. These wooden shoes, imported from the Netherlands, are intended for daily use rather than as souvenirs. While wooden shoes are also worn by the French, Swedes, Danes, Flemish, and others, they are commonly associated with the Dutch. The latest Dutch and Flemish entertainment club to be founded in Essex County has been named the Wooden Shoe Club.

employer should not receive the full blame in all cases because our New Canadians were anxious to work, but in this new country they had no idea of the current value of their services. Working in close harmony with the Unemployment Insurance Commission and the local office of the Department of Immigrants, we were able to stamp out this type of miserable exploitation of our new future citizens.

We also found qualified technicians among our New Canadians, whose specialized knowledge could not be utilized in Windsor .... [Among these was] a Dutch audio engineer whom we finally placed with the Canadian Broadcasting Co. in London.[2]

This Catholic Immigration Centre was located in a former convent in the heart of the factory district. It opened its doors in August 1954. Many members of the Catholic Women's League assisted the St. Vincent de Paul Society in this effort to aid New Canadians:

In 1952, in Windsor, we organized the St. Vincent de Paul Society in our Parishes and early in 1954 our Bishop J.C. Cody, challenged our St. Vincent de Paul Society with the responsibility of taking care of all New Canadians. The Catholic Women's League assisted us in our work and as team mates, with His Excellency as our captain, we established our Catholic Immigration Centre in August, 1954. The Centre was originally a Convent and we could house as many as 65 New Canadians at a time. For the past few years this Centre has been the first Canadian home for over 2,000 New Canadians regardless of race, colour or creed .... When the new arrivals registered at our Centre, it was ascertained what was the Church of their choice. The following morning, the priest, minister, or rabbi, was notified of the new arrivals. Where there was a National Church established, naturally it was the National Church that was notified. Members of the respective Parishes or Congregations would be assigned to visit the New Canadians at the Centre. Many friendships were developed through this program between Old and New Canadians.

The visitors would arrange to take the New Canadians out for drives, picnics, and other activities. Now we found that each Sunday morning, our New Canadians were ready early, for they were being called for by Old Canadians who would take them to Church, and then, in many cases, to their own homes for a Sunday dinner. It is impossible to estimate fully the importance of this early social integration, but I can assure you that many jobs, homes, and other tangible assistance were obtained for our New Canadians through this activity.[3]

Reverend Frans Reuser of Rotterdam was the priest assigned to care for Dutch Roman Catholics in Windsor. He worked closely with a Catholic layman, John Noestheden, one of the first Dutch skilled craftsmen to arrive in Windsor after World War II. Shortly after the war, John Noestheden was employed as a foreman in an airplane factory in the Netherlands, when Prince Bernhard made an official visit to the factory, and spoke with him. Prince Bernhard discovered that John Noestheden was experienced as a cabinetmaker and had training in the repair of fine antique furniture. Concerned about the war damage to some of the priceless antiques in the palace at Soestdijk, Prince Bernhard soon convinced Noestheden to move with his wife and four children to that town. There they lived for seven years while he repaired the royal antiques.

Early in the 1950s the Noesthedens arrived in Windsor, eagerly looking forward to a new life in Canada. They had understood from the Canadian immigration authorities that a house and a job were to be provided. On arrival they found that this was not true, and they were thrown on their own resources. Not yet speaking English, they were at an additional disadvantage. John Noestheden eventually found work as a house painter, and only after three years was he able to find work suited to his abilities.

Through these experiences the Noesthedens understood the plight of the new Dutch immigrants, and offered their assistance to Reverend Frans Reuser in his work at the Catholic Immigration Centre. Although Father Reuser was officially assigned to Immaculate Conception parish, he carried out most of his work in the Centre, where he said Mass and heard confessions in the Dutch language, and gave practical assistance to newly arrived immigrants from the Netherlands.

Father Reuser was also closely associated with an informal group of concerned Windsor citizens. One of these was John Napier, an immigration inspector who took a strong personal interest in the settlement of New Canadians. When he learned that Dutch immigrants were expected to arrive in the city, usually by train from Toronto, John Napier would contact the appropriate welcoming parties. Often, this dedicated group of individuals consisting of Father Reuser, the Levers, and the Knappers, would be found waiting together for their new arrivals at the railway station. The Department of Immigration provided temporary accommodation in tourist cabins for those who could not be housed in the Knappers' own home, or, after 1954, in the Catholic Immigration Centre. The Noestheden family invited Father Reuser, in turn, to their dinner table, for such familiar Dutch specialties as *zuurkool* and *boerenkool met worst*.

Beginning in 1957 the number of immigrants to Windsor dwindled, and many of the organizations connected with the influx were discontinued. Later Dutch arrivals had more opportunities to learn English beforehand, and those who came in the late 1950s frequently benefitted from cash subsidies provided by one of several new emigration societies in the Netherlands.

Now there was no pressing need for emergency measures. Indeed, those who arrived in these later

Chef Glenn Van Blommestein often makes *bitter balletjes* (meatballs) when asked to prepare a typical Dutch dish. They are usually made with veal or chicken and are served as hors d'ouevres at parties or banquets in the Netherlands.

Van Blommestein was born in Leyden, the Netherlands, but as a young child lived in Indonesia, Singapore, and Uruguay while his father served as Ambassador of the Netherlands. When he was 11 years old, the family returned to the Netherlands, where he attended school. As a young man he entered the School of Culinary Arts in Voorhout, a suburb of The Hague, specializing in pastry during his four years of study.

In 1967 Van Blommestein saw a film about Canada that inspired him to emigrate to this country. After a year in London, Ontario, and one year in Vancouver, he travelled to South America, visiting every country on that continent. Later he returned to Ontario and accepted a position with the Food Services Department at St. Clair College in Windsor, and helped found the Windsor Culinary Society, of which he is now co-chairman.

In 1978 his sister Tara Van Blommestein came to Windsor after having spent some years in South America herself. She worked and studied in Windsor before returning to the Hague. She has since taken up residence in Bangladesh where she is attached to the Royal Netherlands Embassy as Secretary, and is in charge of foreign aid. Glenn Van Blommestein still travels extensively and keeps close contact with his family and friends in the Netherlands.

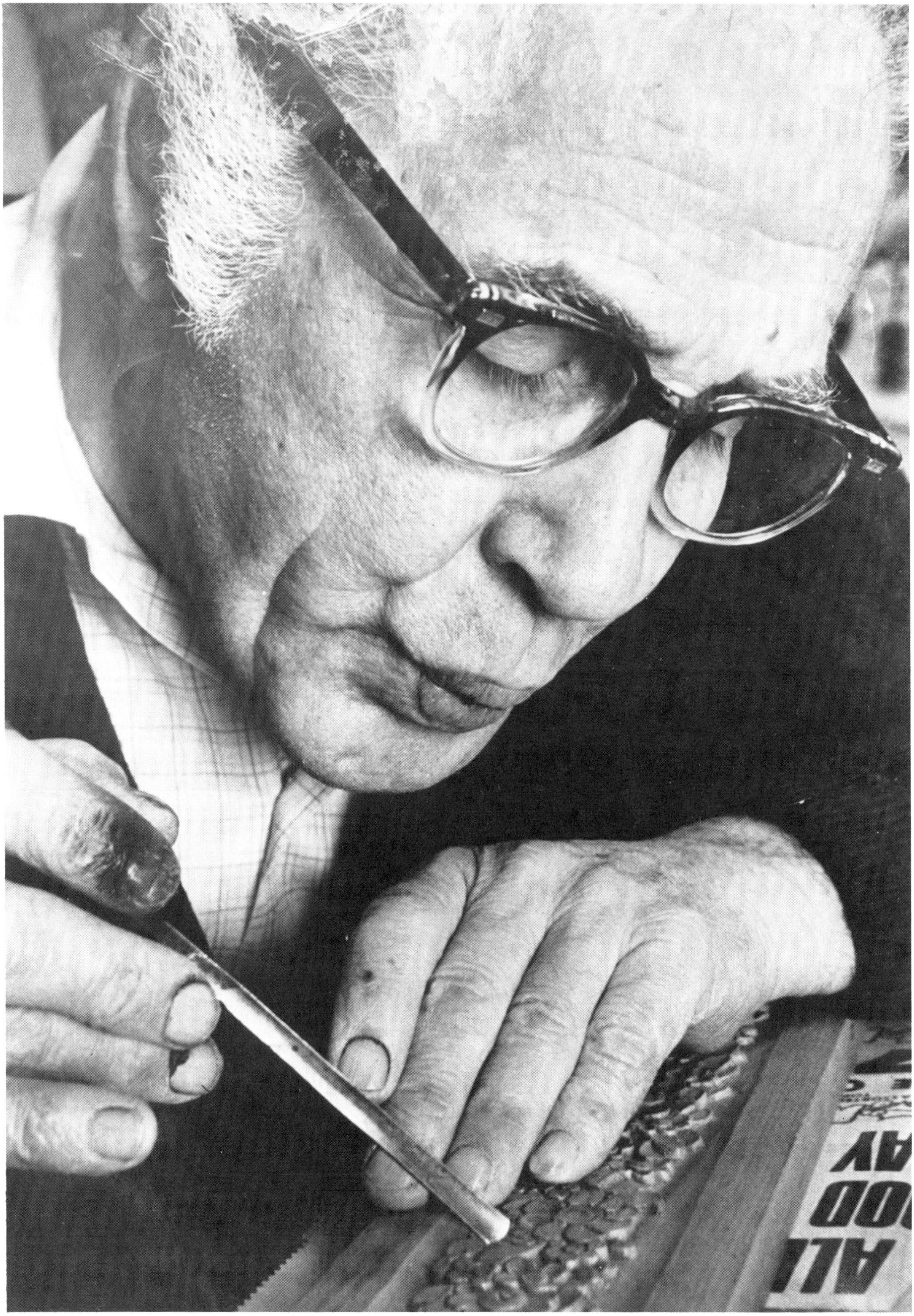

years found that stable Dutch communities had formed in Windsor, Essex, and Leamington, and that there were several hundred of their countrymen ready to welcome newcomers to their organizations.

John Noestheden was still active as a cabinetmaker at the age of 66 when this picture was taken in January 1972. *This photograph was used to illustrate an article which appeared in* The Windsor Star *under the title: "Windsor Cabinetmaker: Last of a Dying Breed." In this article, the interviewer told of a meeting with John Noestheden in the workshop which he built in the renovated garage connected to the family home. There, he had repaired furniture for the 20 years he had been in Canada; work that scarcely used the talents of this fine craftsman, but which allowed him to earn a living for his family as an independent worker with his own business. Both he and his wife Helena assisted other Dutch immigrants settling in Windsor in the 1950s, helping in the programme offered by the Catholic Immigration Centre. Two sons, John and Hank, have become prominent as Ontario artists, with major exhibitions in the last ten years, including one at the Art Gallery of Windsor in June 1976. Their work is found in major collections in Canada, including the art galleries of Windsor and Hamilton, and in several galleries in the United States.*

Rev. Peter de Jong, pastor of both Valetta Presbyterian Church and Faith Reformed Church of Kingsville. *As an immigrant from the Netherlands he trained for the Ministry with the purpose of serving others who had also endured the privations of World War II, the wrenching experience of emigration, and the difficult process of adjustment to life in another country.*

Late in 1950, Faith Reformed Church was established in an old school house on a one-acre lot at Highway 18 and Graham Side Road in Gosfield South. Even then, plans had already been made for a new building, which was completed in 1978. Much of the work was done by church members themselves, some of whom spent hundreds of hours working on the project.

13

The Growth of a Dutch Community:
The Churches

From 1947 onward, Dutch communities were developing in Windsor, Essex, and Leamington, as rural and urban families joined together in a common need of a church of their own denomination with services conducted in the Dutch language. For the Roman Catholics this need was answered for a short time by the work carried out by Father Reuser at the Catholic Immigration Centre and by the Capuchins at St. Mary's Church in Blenheim. Soon, however, these Dutch immigrants joined their local parishes and learned English. Unlike the immigrants of other nationalities, the Dutch, like the Maltese, did not have "national" parishes, and were integrated quickly into the parish life of "Old Canadians". Dutch priests, members of the order Priests of the Sacred Heart, had come to the London and Delaware areas of southwestern Ontario in 1952 to assist with pastoral work among Catholic Dutch immigrants who were plentiful in the region. Their work extended on occasion to Essex County, where they gave pastoral care to some of the recent Dutch immigrants in the 1950s and 1960s. One of the last to work in the County was the Reverend Bernard Ros, who served as an assistant at the Church of St. Simon and St. Jude in Belle River for several years, beginning in 1969.

Already in 1947, with the arrival of the first Dutch farm families, the Knappers had encouraged the re-establishment of a Christian Reformed Church in Windsor. For nearly two years, orthodox Calvinist immigrants met at the Y.M.C.A. in Windsor. When a Christian Reformed Church was founded in Essex in February 1950, it seemed best for members of the smaller Windsor congregation to travel to Essex rather than to establish a permanent church of their own in the city. Since many Dutch immigrants were drawn from farming areas of the Netherlands with a high proportion of orthodox Calvinists, the majority of the newcomers were *Gereformeerd* in the late 1940s and 1950s. Consequently, the church in Essex grew quickly and became firmly established in 1950. It soon became apparent that it would continue to be the largest in Essex County, and would serve as a "mother church" for the area. An attempt to establish a Christian Reformed Church there had been made in 1928 but had failed because most of the Dutch in Essex

77

Rev. Adrian Jansen, director of the Holy Family Retreat House at Oxley (near Lake Erie), one of only two retreat houses in the Roman Catholic Diocese of London. *His father was a court translator of Dutch to English who assisted many Dutch immigrants with their language problems on their arrival in Windsor following World War II.*

County had left for the tobacco fields of Norfolk. The church founded in 1950 was a new one, formed by the immigrants who had arrived after World War II. Their first church building was of brick, bought for $5,500 in 1950.

Many chose to settle in or near Essex precisely because a church of their denomination had been established there. Soon the congregation outgrew the small church and purchased land on the southeast side of Essex. During the years when funds were being collected for a large church, the congregation met in a basement auditorium which was dedicated in 1957. By 1958, a parsonage was completed next to the church site. Plans were already underway for completion of the main structure.

In Leamington still another Christian Reformed congregation was founded. This began to form in 1947 with the arrival of the first Dutch farm families. While the members met in Leamington for many years, in 1963 they decided to join the Essex Church, and its members increased the size of the Essex congregation to such an extent that it was necessary to complete the church as quickly as possible. On 4 March 1965 the church was dedicated, and it became the centre of the activities of the Christian Reformed Church in Essex County.

For several years, Windsor families continued to commute to Essex on Sundays and to attend church meetings there on other occasions. However, as their children grew to school age, the Windsor parents wanted to give them the advantage of attending the Bible School held in the Christian Reformed Church in Essex. Parents began to take turns driving the children to Essex on Saturdays. After more than a year of this, the Windsor parents decided to establish a congregation in the city once again. It was founded in December 1966, and named Ambassador Community Church.

This new church, like many other Christian Reformed ones built in Canada in the 1960s and 1970s, was called a "Community Church" to emphasize openness to members of all nationalities.

The first minister of Ambassador Community Church was the Reverend Dick Kwantas, a missionary of the Christian Reformed Church in Grand Rapids. After two years as minister of the church, he was replaced by the Reverend Hank De Bruin, also from Grand Rapids. After a short stay, this second minister left to carry on missionary work with the native peoples of Canada and the United States. The third minister was the Reverend Peter Hogeterp, a Canadian immigrant of Frisian origin who had immigrated to Canada as a child. His family took part in the Dutch Farm Families movement of the period immediately following World War II. He attended Calvin College in Grand Rapids, where he trained for the ministry. Under his guidance Ambassador Community Church expanded, the congregation growing from a small group of Dutch immigrants to a large, active congregation numbering more than 60 families of many national origins. Dutch immigrants and their families still predominate, but the Dutch language is no longer used in worship services. Encouraged by the spurt of growth brought by the Reverend Peter Hogeterp's ministry to the community at large, the congregation planned a new church building. This was built on the outskirts of Windsor in an area attractive to Dutch immigrants of rural origin, away from the congestion of central Windsor.

Still another group of orthodox Calvinists was represented in Essex County from 1947 onward. These were the members of the strongly orthodox *gereformeerde Kerken, onderhoudende Article 31*. These Calvinists have continued to travel to Chatham on Sundays to attend the services of the Canadian Reformed Church (Article 31). Although few in number, the rural families of Dutch origin who founded this church in Ontario "do their utmost to keep the religious convictions and traditions that they brought over from the Netherlands"[1]:

> The goal is to pass on the spiritual heritage completely free from outside influences to the following generations, born and bred in Canada. To reach this goal the members of this church try to keep the education of their youth completely to themselves, barring outside influences as much as possible.[2]

There were also liberal Calvinists among the farm families who settled in the Leamington area beginning in 1947. For five years, some travelled to Chatham to attend the services of the First Reformed Church. Eventually, they decided to form their own congregation. On 20 July 1952 they held their first service in the home of William van den Berg on Concession 12 in Leamington.

As more Dutch immigrants arrived, it became necessary to rent quarters for the growing congregation. Church services were held in a hall in Leamington until 1957, when the church moved to its permanent location on Highway 18 at Albertville, six miles west of Leamington. The congregation bought an old country school house from the School Board of Gosfield South Township and converted it into a small country church.

During the earliest years of the group's existence, the early 1950s, religious services were conducted by the minister of the Chatham church, the Reverend Herman Maassen. When officially organized as Faith Reformed Church on 18 October 1955, the group became a congregation of the Reformed Church in America, with the Reverend Gerrit Molenaar as minister from 1955 to 1958. Reverend Ralph van der Pol served from 1958 to 1965, followed by Pastor Richard van Farowe from 1965 to 1968, when the church was without a minister for a year. Reverend Peter De Jong became the fourth minister of the church, and has continued in that position since 1969. He also became the minister of Valetta Presbyterian Church, a small country church which remained Pres-

The Reverend Jurrien Camman, minister of Riverside United Church since 1974. *The Reverend Camman has been actively associated with other clergymen of Netherlandic origin during his Windsor ministry, assisting at special services held in both Dutch and English to mark such occasions as the thirty-fifth anniversary of the liberation of the Netherlands. In 1983 there were no fewer than 11 clergymen of Dutch origin active in Essex County.*

byterian in 1925 when most of the other Presbyterian churches of Essex County joined with Methodist and Congregational churches to form the United Church of Canada.

In his position as minister of the two churches, Reverend De Jong served on both church boards and committees for both the Presbyterian Church of Canada and the Reformed Church in America at the national level. At the local level, he preached three times each Sunday. He preached in English at the morning service of Faith Reformed Church, and then repeated this sermon in Valetta, 32 miles away. In the afternoon he gave a sermon in Dutch at Faith Reformed Church in Kingsville, for the benefit of older members of the congregation, in particular the immigrants for whom this church was founded. Reverend De Jong has been a strong supporter of ecumenism, and commented recently:

> Some of us as churches stand miles apart from each other, and I think it's really that we just don't know each other .... That is one of the sad things about church history — we have separated the body of Christ into so many different organisms that for the non-Christian it is so difficult to determine who is the real Christian.[3]

Many liberal Calvinist immigrants joined Presbyterian or United Church of Canada congregations when they came to Essex County after World War II. However, a small number wanted a church of their own that conducted services in Dutch. Ministers from the Reformed Church in America had been providing these services in the area for some time, since both the United and Presbyterian churches had not responded to their need.

Reverend Hans Zegerius was the assistant minister of St. Andrew's Presbyterian Church in Windsor for four years in the 1960s, and among those who helped establish in Canada the Reformed Church in America:

> Post-World War II immigration from the Netherlands brought to Canada many Protestants steeped in the Netherland's Reformed tradition. In 1948, the first meeting of a group of Reformed immigrants was held in the People's Church in Hamilton, Ontario. A few months later they made a request to the Board of Domestic Missions of the Reformed Church in America to establish a mission in Hamilton which could provide for the spiritual needs of Dutch immigrants of Reformed background. Subsequently, this group joined the Reformed Church in America, and, in 1950, Reverend Zegerius was installed as pastor of the first Reformed Church of Hamilton.[4]

Reverend Zegerius founded the official Canadian church journal of the Reformed Church in America in 1951. First called *Monthly for New Canadians from Holland*, and then *Pioneer: Monthly for Netherlanders in the New World*, it is now known as the *Pioneer: Christian Monthly*.

In 1969, Reverend Adrian Jansen became director of the Holy Family Retreat House on Highway 18A in Oxley, near Harrow. He immigrated with his mother and brothers and sisters in 1929 when he was ten years old. His father, Peter Jansen, had come to Canada from Rotterdam two years earlier, and had settled in Toronto. However, by the time his wife and children joined him, the depression had commenced and immigration authorities directed the reunited family to Windsor, where they remained. Peter Jansen was a Catholic layman who was one of the founders of the Catholic Immigration Service, active in the 1950s. Dutch was spoken often in the Jansen home, and the older children of the family retained their spoken Dutch. Father Jansen received his seminary training as a diocesan priest in St. Peter's Seminary in London, Ontario. Before becoming director of the retreat house, he taught for ten years at Brennan High School, was chaplain at Hotel Dieu Hospital in Windsor for four years, and served as a curate and priest at various churches.

Reverend J. Camman, now minister of Riverside United Church, arrived in Canada in 1955 from The Hague, as a young man of twenty. He was sponsored by his brother who was living in Winnipeg. After seven years at United College in Winnipeg, beginning in 1956, he graduated as a minister of the United Church of Canada. His first pastoral charges were in northwestern Ontario and Manitoba. From there, he went to Edmonton, Alberta, and after serving in two churches there, came to Windsor in 1974.

Another Windsor minister, Reverend Peter Melleghers, came to Canada from Vlaardigen, near Rotterdam, in 1953 and settled in Toronto. After some years as an importer of Dutch food products, he decided to enter the ministry. He took his undergraduate training at Calvin College and his seminary training at Knox College in Toronto. After serving as minister in various rural churches in Ontario, he came to Windsor in 1979 as minister of Riverside Presbyterian Church.

In 1982 Rev. Bernard M. Bouwmeester became minister of Sandwich United Church, Windsor. He had immigrated to Canada with his wife in 1951, settling in Stoney Creek (near Hamilton). After working in construction and as a sign painter and later advertising manager of a large department store, he entered McMaster University to do undergraduate work. In 1970, he graduated from Emmanuel College, University of Toronto. In the early 1970s he was minister of Woodslee United Church. After some years in Wallaceburg, he returned to Essex County to become the minister of Sandwich United Church.

Still another denomination, the Folk Gospel Ministry, represented in Essex County by Ebenezer Church in the town of Essex, has as its minister a Dutch immigrant, Rev. N. Prinsen.

Rev. Vincent Van Zutphen was head of the Ontario Regional Catholic Charismatic Conference held in July 1983 at the University of Windsor and in Cleary Auditorium in Windsor. *Nearly 6,000 Roman Catholics attended from across Ontario and the United States.*

Father Van Zutphen was born in Keldonk; he lived there and in Mariahout in North Brabant, the Netherlands, before emigrating to Canada with his family in 1951. He continued his highschool education in Blenheim, Ontario. His family later moved to Nova Scotia.

Rev. Van Zutphen became a member of the Order of St. Augustine in the late 1950s and was ordained a priest in 1963. In 1973 he received a Ph.D. in scripture studies from the University of Wurzburg, West Germany. He is now a teacher at St. Peter's Seminary in London, Ontario.

Dick Nieuwland (left) and Herman Schinkel outside the newly established Essex County Christian School in 1976. *Together with about 60 Essex County families, these two men helped establish a Christian school within the county for their children to attend. Previously, many of their children travelled to Chatham to attend a Christian school. The school was founded in conjunction with the National Union of Christian Schools, an organization of about 300 private schools which share a similar Christian philosophy.*

Each year the Dutch Canadian Society — Neerlandia of Essex County holds a "Sinterklaas" party to let children of Dutch and Flemish origin enjoy the customs which surround the celebration of the feast-day of St. Nicholas or "Sinterklaas," one of the most popular of all Dutch celebrations. *The main festivities take place on the eve of December 6, St. Nicholas Day. For centuries, that night has been an occasion for gatherings and giving gifts to children and other family members.*

According to the most popular legend, the "Good Saint" appears on that evening dressed as a bishop, and carrying a golden crozier. He rides a white horse and is accompanied by a Moorish boy, Black Peter, who carries a bag of presents for good children, and lumps of coal for naughty ones. Special traditional delicacies are served, and "Sinterklaas songs" are sung by the entire family, who all enter into the spirit of this popular children's celebration. Neerlandia holds its Sinterklaas party on the weekend preceding December 6, when the children and their parents gather to sing St. Nicholas songs and to be present for the impressive visit of the Saint.

14

Dutch Social Clubs

The first of the local social organizations to be formed was named "Neerlandia". It began in 1957 under the direction of Hendrik de Laat of Maidstone Township. A drama group, its members included technicians, skilled craftsmen, and their wives. The majority of these participants had arrived in the early 1950s from urban areas. They met for three years, and presented a number of plays quite successfully. One of these was *Anne Frank*, based on the book *The Diary of Anne Frank*, set in wartime Amsterdam. Neerlandia thus carried on the tradition of a pre-World War II immigrant theatre group which presented plays in the Dutch language. This group, the Vlaanderen's Kerels, was founded by Flemings and presented traditional morality plays for entertainment. Popular were patriotic Flemish dramas and classical works by Joost van den Vondel.

The post-war drama society was comparable to the many amateur theatre groups popular in the 1950s, both in Canada and the Netherlands. Membership in this theatre group was open to persons of any religious group.

Soon after Neerlandia began to produce plays, a soccer team was formed. The first president of the Neerlandia soccer team, Hendrik Spaandonk, aroused great enthusiasm for the game among the players and their wives. To raise money for accident insurance and uniforms, Neerlandia sponsored dances, and held them at the Goodfellows Hall on Campbell Avenue in Windsor. Unfortunately, prohibitive costs and a number of accidents made it necessary to disband the team after three successful years.

Neerlandia continued to meet through the 1960s. Members played games including table tennis and billiards, and *Klaverjassen* was especially popular. A Hamilton, Ontario, immigrant, G. W. Graaskamp, wrote:

> The most popular Dutch card game is called "klaverjassen" and it is played enthusiastically, sometimes fanatically, by very many in the Netherlands and now also in Canada. Whenever a bunch of Dutchmen get together it appears that some of them start to "klaverjas". Considering their numbers here it is not surprising that these cardplayers organized themselves; there are at least 9 clubs: in Woodstock, London, Cambridge, Kitchener, Toronto, Hamilton, Georgetown, Oshawa, and St. Catherines. These clubs together

Thea Brouwer and Veronica Veldhuis join Maj. Jock MacLellan in commemorating the twenty-fifth anniversary of the liberation of the Netherlands by Canadian troops. *Major MacLellan took part in the liberation while serving with the Essex Scottish Regiment.*

form a federation that regularly organizes tournaments, usually 6 a year, where about 250 players take part .... Considering the very Dutch nature of the game it is not surprising that all players, except for a very few ... are Dutch. Klaverjassen is certainly something specifically Dutch; maybe it can be called part of the Dutch culture.[1]

During the 1960s, Neerlandia was in contact with other Dutch social clubs in Canada and received news of their plans and activities. In 1970 all of these clubs joined in a special tribute to Canada which was called "Thank you, Canada",[2] as part of the celebration of the twenty-fifth anniversary of the liberation of the Netherlands by the Canadian Armed Forces in 1945. By their efforts, the Dutch social clubs of Canada collected a total of $120,000, and used it to purchase a magnificent organ, which was presented to Canada at a special commemorative service. Over $4,000 was collected in Windsor by Neerlandia, whose members went door-to-door, asking for contributions from Essex County residents with Dutch names. Some of those who contributed were not recent arrivals, but descendants of the United Empire Loyalists bearing common Dutch names. Since the Essex Scottish Regiment played a significant role in the liberation of the Netherlands, there was much local interest in the Windsor celebration. On this occasion, William Holzel, as president of Neerlandia, presented a commemorative plaque to Judge Bruce McDonald, commander of the Essex Scottish Regiment.

In the late 1960s and early 1970s Neerlandia became a large society of 300 to 400 members. This growth was chiefly due to the low-priced charter flights to Amsterdam which were available to those who joined the society. Betsy Wigcherink, formerly of Haarlem, the Netherlands, was in charge of charter flights for the group. In 1975 a second society led by William Holzel also provided charter flights as one of its main attractions for members. This group was called the Holland-Canada Association, Windsor District. As well as special charter flights for Carnival and Christmas, summer flights were offered. This society also offered charter trips to the annual tulip festival held in Holland, Michigan. There, descendants of the Seceders of the nineteenth century had established a festival to celebrate their Dutch heritage. The Holland-Canada Society continued to meet for a few years in the 1970s before the two groups were amalgamated to form, once again, a single society: "Dutch Canadian Society-Neerlandia".

In the late 1970s, interest in charter flights declined as travel costs increased. Membership in Neerlandia dropped, but interest among remaining members stayed high. These meetings took many forms but always included games, dances, and an annual banquet. There were two bowling leagues, and until 1981 a "klaverjas club". At its parties, Neerlandia always featured typical Dutch specialties such as *bitterballen* (a type of meatball) and raw herring. From time to time the club members attended special film programmes of interest to the Dutch presented at the Windsor Public Library. These events sometimes attracted more than 300 people, to view such films as *It Wasn't Easy*, a National Film Board presentation on Dutch immigration to Canada, and *Juliana 70*, a film portrait of Queen Juliana of the Netherlands in her seventieth year.

In 1980 the Dutch societies of Canada presented a quilt to Queen Juliana on the occasion of her seventieth birthday. A Toronto Dutch society planned this gesture whereby each club prepared a square of the quilt, embroidered with a provincial flower of Canada. These were sent to the Toronto group whose members assembled the quilt, and sent a delegation to the Netherlands to present it to Queen Juliana. Fondness and respect for Queen Juliana (now Princess Juliana), who spent the war years in Ottawa, is a common bond between the Dutch women immigrants to Canada. A certificate which recognizes the contribution made by Neerlandia to Queen Juliana's seventieth birthday gift is a prized possession of the society.

Each year the society publishes several issues of *Neerlandia News* to announce the programmes planned for the season. These booklets also include poems and brief news articles. Neerlandia exchanges these newsletters with the other Dutch societies in Canada, and with a similar Dutch-American organization in Detroit. The Windsor society is patterned after one of the Canadian groups, with which it maintains particularly close contacts: Club the Netherlands of St. Catharines, Ontario.

In 1982 the society officially celebrated the twenty-fifth anniversary of its founding. On March 6 of that year an "Old Dutch Village Market" was held in the Croatian Centre in Windsor. This colourful event drew over 700 visitors during the day. Many were Dutch immigrants, but there were also many members of the community at large, drawn by the prospect of shopping at the market. That evening, the society held its anniversary banquet and dance. Among others, Julian Wigcherink, president of Neerlandia, and Betsy Wigcherink, two of the founders, were honoured at the banquet. A second "Old Dutch Village Market" was held in March 1983, and was equally successful, so that it promises to become an annual event.

In 1974 a Dutch society known as the Wooden Shoe Club was begun in Leamington, and one of the founding members of this group was Fred Evers, who came to Kingsville from Hensbroek in North Holland in 1967 as a young man of 20. The Wooden Shoe Club's location put it within a reasonable travelling distance from the areas around Kingsville and Leamington, where many Dutch and Belgian farmers are engaged in market gardening and horticulture. Membership in the Wooden Shoe Club immediately reached 175, and has stayed large, ensuring the existence of the society for some time to come. A number of the most enthusiastic members have also joined Neerlandia in Windsor.

On Saturday, 6 March 1982, the Dutch Canadian Society — Neerlandia celebrated its twenty-fifth anniversary with a formal banquet and dance. Henk De Laat, Vice President of the society, is seen reading the text of a commemorative plaque presented to Julian Wigcherink, President, in recognition of the important contribution that he and Betsy Wigcherink have made to the continued growth and success of the society. Seen from left to right are: William Holzel, fifth president of Neerlandia; Mrs. René De Seranno; René De Seranno, Consul of Belgium in Detroit, Michigan; Julian Wigcherink, seventh president of Neerlandia; Henk De Laat; Betsy Wigcherink, Secretary of Neerlandia; Dr. O. Akkerman, Hon. Vice Consul for the Netherlands, Chatham, Ontario.

Betsy Wigcherink, secretary of the Dutch Canadian Society — Neerlandia, and editor of the *Neerlandia News*, holding the society's copy of the certificate announcing the gift of a quilt to Queen Juliana of the Netherlands on her seventieth birthday. *On the document is a list of Dutch-Canadian societies which took part in creating the quilt, on which were embroidered the floral emblems of Canada.*

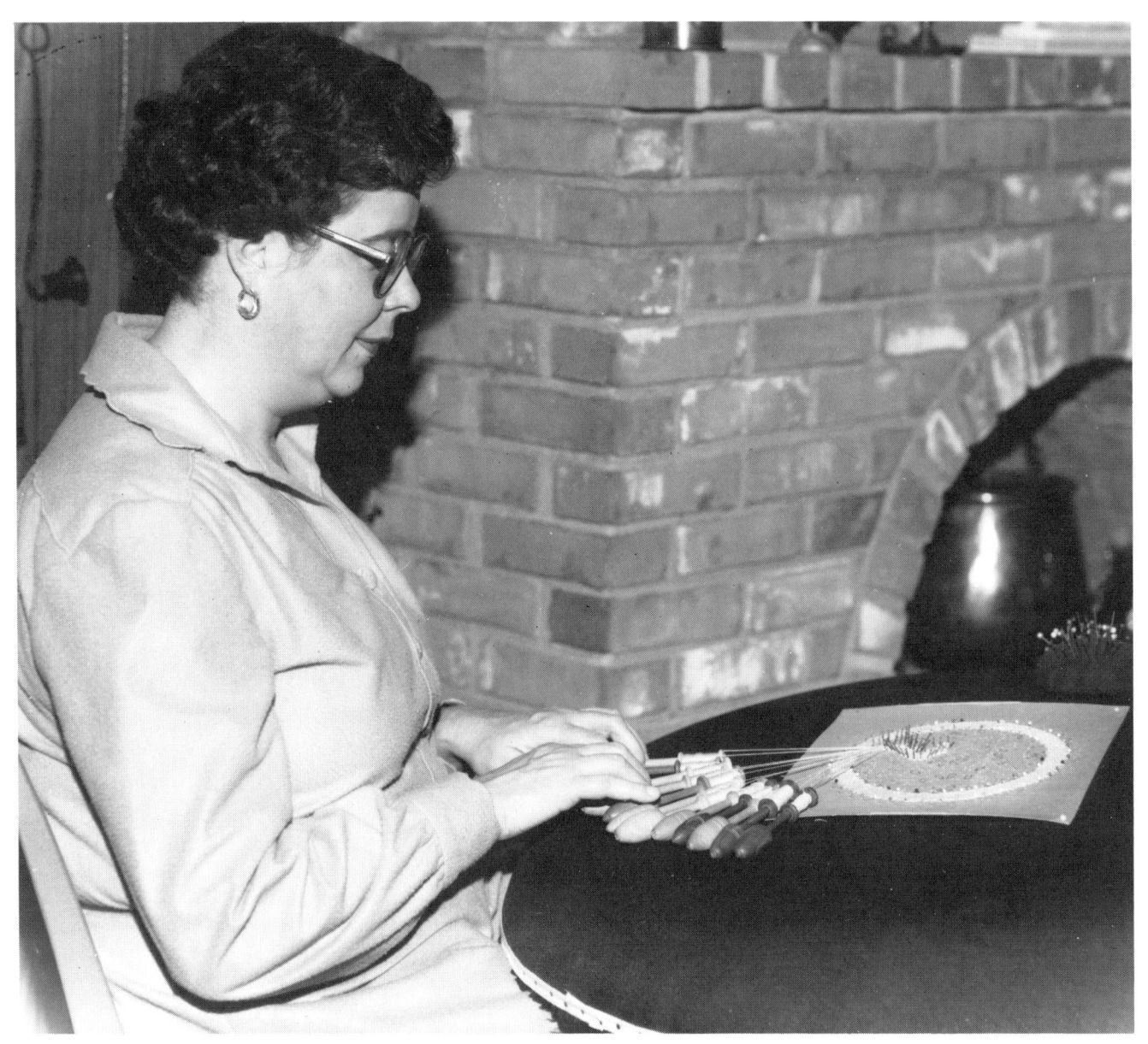

Brigitte McFadden is studying the traditional art of lacemaking. As Brigitte Vanaudenaerde she arrived in Canada with her brother and her parents from her native West Flanders. She was born in Ardooie, not far from Bruges, in an area noted for its fine handmade lace. Brigitte is using the lace bobbins once used by her own grandmother, an accomplished lacemaker.

Brigitte has been very active as a member of the executive of Neerlandia, serving as treasurer and helping establish the Old Dutch Village Market as an annual event. She is an elementary school teacher in the separate schools of Windsor and recently earned the degree of Master of Education at the University of Windsor. She has been instrumental in keeping alive the traditions of Flanders in Windsor, introducing her students to the St. Nicholas celebration and a commemorative programme entitled "In Flanders Fields".

Jenny Burridge came to Canada with her family as a teenager, and has since retained her knowledge of the Dutch language which she reads, writes, and speaks with fluency. *Together with Sylvia Thijs she assisted with the preparation of this book by interviewing residents of Essex County who were born in the Netherlands. Here she is seen in her Windsor home, which is decorated in keeping with her Dutch heritage. Among the family treasures is this lovely nineteenth-century Dutch watercolour of a Frisian woman in her regional costume.*

The mayor of Essex, Jerry Schinkel, his wife Ruth, and Essex businessman Jim Barnett watch results of the voting after an election held November 1982. Schinkel was returned to office by a three-to-two margin over a former mayor Ed Michael.

Schinkel became mayor in 1980 after serving as reeve of the town. He immigrated from Utrecht shortly after World War II, settling near other members of his family in Essex County. His father was closely associated with the Christian Reformed Church of Essex which he helped to establish in the 1950s.

Mayor Schinkel has been an established businessman in Essex for many years. Dutch cheese, meats, and other specialties of the Netherlands are a particular feature of his popular market.

15

The Dutch In Essex County In The 1980s:
A Survey

The year 1982 marked not only the twenty-fifth anniversary of the founding of Neerlandia but also the thirty-fifth anniversary of the arrival of the first Dutch post-war immigrants in 1947. Approximately 90% of the Dutch in Essex County arrived in Canada before 1960, when immigration from the Netherlands was at its height.

Many of the Dutch immigrants to Essex County have moved elsewhere in Canada and cannot easily be traced. Others have returned to the Netherlands to live. Some of those now living in the county have also returned to the Netherlands, only to come back to Canada once again, unable to readjust to life there. Those living in Essex County, like other postwar Dutch immigrants in Canada, are not cut off from events in their homeland, but are fully aware of the great changes that have taken place in all aspects of society and life since they left for Canada. Through letters from friends and relatives, newspapers and journals, they hear about the disadvantages and advantages of life in the 1980s in the Netherlands.

It seems appropriate now, in this anniversary year, for Dutch immigrants still living in Essex County to look back on their immigration experience and their years in Canada. With this in mind, in the spring of 1982, two members of the Dutch community, Sylvia Thijs and Jenny Burridge, interviewed 100 Dutch immigrants in their homes. Each was asked to answer a questionnaire.[1]

Question 1 asked for current place of residence by city or town and province; and for place of birth, city or town, province or county.

Of the 100 people interviewed[2] (54) lived in Windsor and (46) in other parts of the County of Essex. They have immigrated from all provinces of the Netherlands except Zeeland, the province from which so many of the Dutch had come to Essex County in the years 1910-1930. The provinces of origin of those surveyed in 1982 are as follows:

Province	Residents Windsor	Residents Outside Windsor	Total
Groningen	1	—	1
Friesland	4	8	12
Drente	2	3	5
Overijssel	6	2	8
Gelderland	1	4	5
Utrecht	7	4	11
North Holland	9	5	14
South Holland	11	8	19
Zeeland	—	—	—
North Brabant	5	8	13
Limburg	5	—	5
Indonesia	3	—	3
No answer	—	4	4
	54	46	100

Percentage of Urbanization by Province

Province	Remained rural	Remained urban	Rural to urban	Urban to rural
Groningen	—	—	1	—
Friesland	6	3	3	—
Drente	1	—	4	—
Overijssel	2	4	2	—
Gelderland	4	1	—	—
Utrecht	1	4	6	—
North Holland	3	8	1	2
South Holland	4	6	7	2
Zeeland	—	—	—	—
North Brabant	6	1	4	2
Limburg	—	1	4	—
Indonesia	—	3	—	—
No answer	4	—	—	—
	31	31	32	6

Question 2 *asked of the people born outside Canada how they came to the country.* [The answer to this question has been integrated with that to Question 7.]

Question 3 *asked about citizenship.* Of the 100 surveyed, (95) have become naturalized Canadian citizens; (4) remain Dutch citizens; (1) is an American citizen.

Question 4 *asked: If you are a naturalized Canadian citizen or plan to become one, please give the reasons.*

All but seven answered, some giving two or three reasons for taking out citizenship papers. Although the wording varies, the comments can be grouped into five basic responses.
1. For the future of my children. (25)
2. Because I intend to stay in Canada, and wanted the citizen's right to vote. (81)
3. Because my children are here, and I want to belong here, too. (20)
4. For family reasons. (Husband was Canadian or parents made family decision.) (11)
5. To have the right to pensions, government jobs, education. (3)

Responses 1, 2, and 3 were repeated frequently, expressed in many ways.

Question 5 *asked: If you have a landed immigrant status, but are unsure about becoming a Canadian citizen, or do not plan to become one, please give the reasons.*

Two of the four who stated they had retained Dutch citizenship explained it was to prevent loss of pension rights in the Netherlands. One, now an American citizen, stated: "I have already changed from Dutch to U.S. citizenship. Once is enough, if I can help it!"

Question 6 *asked how long the individual had been living in Canada.*

The great majority, (64), have lived in Canada for 21 to 30 years. Another (23) have lived in Canada more than 31 years. Of those who had come more recently, (6) have been in Canada 11-30 years, another (6) from 6-10 years, and only one for "up to five years". A total of (87) have lived in Canada 21 years or more.

Question 7— *When did you arrive in Canada as an immigrant?* — incorporates also the answers from Question 2. The table below shows years of peak immigration.

Year of arrival	Sponsored	Independent	Total
1932	—	1	1
1947	2	1	3
1948	4	—	4
1950	—	1	1
1951	10	4	14
1952	10	9	19
1953	10	6	16
1954	2	9	11
1955	5	3	8
1956	4	—	4
1957	2	2	4
1958	1	—	1
1959	1	2	3
1963	1	—	1
1966	—	1	1
1967	—	1	1
1969	—	2	2
1972	1	2	3
1974	—	1	1
1980	—	1	1
No answer	—	1*	1
	53	47	100

*Came as a visitor & was sponsored later.

Question 8 asked: *Did you have friends or relatives in Canada before you made the decision to immigrate?*

Of the total, (65) had friends or relatives here, (35) did not.

Question 9 asked *age at the time of immigration.*

14 or less (7); 15-20 (19); 21-35 (48); 36-50 (24); 51-64, (none); 65 or older (1); one no answer.

Question 10 asked *if the immigrant had obtained advice, before coming to Canada, from a wide range of organizations.*

The Catholic Central Emigration Foundation (Katholieke Centrale Emigratie Stichting) helped (13); Christian Emigration Centre (Christelijke Emigratie Stichting) (14); General Emigration Centre (Algemene Emigratie Centrale) (27); Protestant Emigration Foundation (Gereformeerde Emigratie Stichting, Ger. Art. 31) (3); State Labour Office (Gewestelijke Arbeidsbureaus) (36).

Question 11 asked *from which sources, if any, the immigrant received help when he arrived in Canada.*

Listed were relatives (40); Dutch friends (25); persons from my hometown (6); Dutch organizations in Canada (3); other (11); none of the above (21).

The various kinds of help mentioned fall into the broad categories of shelter, assistance in writing letters and filling out application forms, introduction to friends, and help in finding a job.

Question 12 asked *about occupation before immigration.*

Homemaker (19); farmer (9); student (9); saleslady (7); registered nurse (5); toolmaker (4); secretary (3); truck driver (3); kindergarten teacher (1); bookkeeper (2); house painter and paper hanger (2); social worker (1); flower-grower (1); welder (1); steam-fitter (1); farmhand (1); pipe-fitter (1); florist (1); draftsman (1); watchmaker (1); midwife (1); tanner (1); electrician (1); service engineer (1); sailor (1); laboratory technician (1); businessman (1); labourer (1); radio technician (1); dental technician (1); dental assistant (1); construction worker (1); design engineer (1); accountant (1); carpenter (1); graduate engineer (1); butcher (1); auto mechanic (1); no answer (9).

Question 13 asked *how the immigrant considered his financial situation in the "old country" before coming to Canada.*

Answers included: below average (15); average (64); above average (12); wealthy (1); no answer (8).

Question 14: *To which city or town did you go when you first came to Canada? Why did you go there?*

Cities and towns in Essex County included: Windsor (32); Leamington (6); Essex (6); Amherstburg (2); Kingsville (2); Harrow (3); Woodslee (1); Malden Centre (1); Sandwich (1); Ruthven (1). Some listed cities and towns in other Canadian provinces: Halifax (1); Edmonton (3); Montreal (2); Charlottetown (1); Woodstock, N.B. (1); Hoey, Sask. (1); Settlement in other places in Ontario included: Sundridge (1); Blenheim (3); Dresden (1); Hamilton (3); Port Perry (1); St. Catherines (1); Guelph (1); Fruitland (1); Ridgetown (1); Paris (1); Fletcher (1); Brampton (1); Chatham (5); Sarnia (3); Highgate (2); Toronto (4); Beamsville (1); Palmyra (1); no answer (4).

Answers to why they settled there can be grouped into several general categories.
1. Relatives living there. (40)
2. Directed by the Canadian Immigration service. (14)
3. Sponsor lived there. (11)
4. Found work there. (11)
5. Had friends there. (10)
6. To get married, fiance lived there. (4)

Other reasons included familiarity because of a former stay; coincidence; and directed there by church.

Mary Verbeek with her daughter Heidi, age eight, at the PET computer terminal, Kingsville Public School. *In January 1983, parents were invited to visit the school to be introduced to the use of the video-display terminal in their children's education. Heidi's father is Matheus (Martin) Verbeek, who was born in the Netherlands in 1948 and came to Essex County with his family as a child of five. They settled on Pelee Island, where his father was employed at the Pioneer Seed plant for some 30 years.*

Question 15 asked religious affiliation.

Christian Ref. Church (25); Reformed Church (10); Roman Catholic Church (28); other (28); no answer (3); none (6).

Question 16 asked how religious beliefs influence the immigrant's way of life.

Religion influences most of my behaviour (34); religion influences some of my behaviour (39); religion does not influence my behaviour (21); no answer (6).

Question 17: Do you take part in any of the activities or organizations of your church other than attending services?

Yes (36); no (62); no answer (2).

Question 18: If you take part in any of the activities or organizations of your Church, what kind of activities of organizations are these?

Of the 36 who take part in the activities or organizations (17) belong to service clubs (8) to study clubs (4) teach religion (7) belong to a consistory or church board (14) engage in family-oriented activities, women's groups, sing in a choir, or serve as an elder.

Question 19: What place does religion take in your life now as compared with the place of religion in your life before you came to Canada?

For (26), it is more important; for (52) it plays the same role as before; for (11), it is less important; (11) gave no answer.

Question 20: Are you living in an urban (population over 5000) or in a rural (population below 5000) area?

Urban areas (63); rural areas (37).

Question 21 asked how much formal education the immigrant had, both in Holland and Canada.

All had completed elementary school: (98) in Holland; (7) in Canada; (1) in Indonesia. Some had a few years of high school: (17) in Holland; (5) in Canada. A larger number had a high school diploma: (19) in Holland; (1) in Canada; (1) in the U.S.; (1) in Indonesia.

A number had some college or university education: (13) in Holland; (11) in Canada; (2) in the U.S. A few had completed college or university: (3) in Holland; (5) in Canada; (2) in the U.S.

A number also had trade school education: (10) in Holland; (1) in Canada.

The figures reflect a strong interest in further education among many of the Dutch in Essex County. A total of (7) of the immigrants have received degrees from Canadian or American college or universities, while another (13) have taken some college or university courses in Canada or the U.S. Many Windsor citizens commute to Detroit for college and university studies, which may well be a factor in the number who report having studied in the U.S. The (12) who had attended various types of specialized trade schools pointed out the omission of this category in the questionnaire, and this information was duly recorded.

Question 21 also asked for information on diploma or degree, the institution, the year, and the area of specialty.

Those obtained in the Netherlands can all be grouped as certificates and degrees leading to professional training for a variety of occupations. The degrees listed as obtained in Canada or the U.S. include: Bachelor of Civil Engineering, University of Michigan, 1957; B.A., University of Windsor, 1976, home economics; PhD, McMaster University, 1960, physics; B.Sc., Detroit Institute of Technology, 1978, chemistry; B.A., University of Rochester, 1951, psychology; M.A. Case-Western Reserve, Cleveland, Ohio, 1953, psychology; B.A., University of Windsor, 1971, German Literature; M.A. University of Toronto, 1973, German literature; Master of Library Science, University of Toronto, 1976.

Question 22: What kind of work did you do when you came to Canada?

The answers were extremely varied, and all are included here. Homemaking (21); housework (14); farming (13); farmhand (3); student (6); long-distance truck driving (3); factory work (4); construction (3); welding (3). Other occupations, listed once each, include: biologist, office work, engineering, design engineering, steamfitting, interior decorator, travel agent, house painting, ladies' fashions, butcher, teacher, flower growing, maternity nursing assistant, laboratory assistant, electrician, labourer, servicing weighscale, instrument maker, saleslady, pipefitter, gardener, tool and die maker, florist, dental technician, landscaping, bank clerk, nursing, kindergarten teacher, dry-cleaning, no answer.

Question 23: What is your occupation at the moment?

A total of (16) people report they are now retired; (37) list themselves as "housewife" or "homemaker"; (6) as farmers; (4) as contractors; (2) as self-employed; and (2) as truckdrivers. The other occupations listed, once each, are: toolmaker, diemaker, interior decorator, student, steamfitter, pipefitter, civil engineer, contractor, singer, factory worker, moldmaker, draftsman, grain elevator operator, construction company owner, daycare teacher, teacher, design engineer, mechanical designer, security man, saleslady, salesman, librarian, chemist, physics professor, electronics technician, businessman, cable splicer, bus driver, psychiatric nurse, registered nursing assistant, house painter, bank worker, landscaper.

Question 24: *What were your important motives for immigration?* Please check your three most important motives; indicate first, second and third choice.

Some (22) list relatives in Canada; (38) a desire to have their own business or farm; (39) the future of their children; (8) financial problems; (18) housing problems; (5) unemployment in the Netherlands; (1) family problems; none, religious reasons; (35) adventure.

Among other reasons listed were: a better future for myself (4); no choice, I went with my parents (4); I followed my husband (4); overpopulation (2); bureaucracy in Holland (2); husband could not find work in U.S.; fear of another war; it was a bad time in Holland.

Question 25: *Do you plan to reside permanently in Canada or do you intend to go back to the "old country"?* (check one).

The vast majority (95), plan to reside permanently in Canada; (1) intends to go back to the "old country"; (4) are undecided.

Five basic reasons are listed for staying in Canada:
1. The immigrant has adjusted, and considers Canada home, e.g. "I have set my roots."
2. Immediate family now Canadian: e.g. "My family could not adjust to Dutch life; myself, I could, and would not mind going back, but my husband and children are Canadians."
3. A liking for Canada: e.g. "Because I feel blessed and privileged to live in this wonderful country."
4. Concern about overpopulation in the Netherlands.
5. A belief that Canada offers more opportunity for the future than does the Netherlands.

Question 26 *asks about the immigrant's satisfaction with his life and job in Canada.*

Some (85) say they are satisfied; (4) are undecided; (9) are dissatisfied; (2) give no answer.

Question 27 *asks whether the immigrant thinks he has risen or fallen in status compared with his status before immigration.*

More than half (62), feel they have risen in status; (28) feel they have remained the same; (3) feel they have fallen; (7) have no answer.

Question 28: *Have you ever returned to visit the Netherlands? If "Yes," what year did you visit the "old country" last?*

No (9); yes, once (13); yes, twice (16); yes, three times (17); yes, four times (7); yes, five or more times (35); no answer (3).

Although the questionnaire was answered in the spring of 1982, already seven had been to the Netherlands in that year. By year: 1982 (7); 1981 (20); 1980 (6); 1979 (7); 1978 (7); 1977 (5); 1976 (2); 1975 (4); 1974 (3); 1973 (1); 1972 (2); 1971 (2); 1970 (3); 1969 (3); 1968 (1); 1965 (2); 1956 (1); no answer (24).

Of those who answered they had never visited the old country (3) said they planned to in the near future; (3) replied no, and (3) gave no answer.

Question 29: *Do you correspond with relatives or friends in the "old country"?*

No (6); yes, but rarely (12); yes, occasionally (20); yes, frequently (31); yes, very frequently (31).

Question 30: *Have you ever assisted or sponsored any relatives or friends from the "old country" to immigrate to Canada?*

No (74); yes, once or twice (20); yes, three or four times (3); yes, five or more times (1); no answer (2).

Question 31: *Do you send money to relatives in the "old country"?*

No (90); yes, but rarely (6); yes, occasionally (4); yes, regularly (none).

Question 32: *How well do you know the Dutch, English and French languages?*

Dutch: very well (80); well (18); not so well (1); very little (1); not at all (none).

English: very well (55); well (45); not so well (none); very little (none); not at all (none).

French: very well (none); well (1); not so well (10); very little (24); not at all (41); no answer (24).

Question 33: *What language do you normally use at home?*

English only (29); most English, some Dutch (40); English and Dutch equal (11); most Dutch, some English (18); Dutch only (2). Other (explain): Frisian; Limburg dialect; German; the children use French.

Question 34: *Do you use the Dutch language at home?*

No (18); yes, but rarely (15); yes, occasionally (29); yes, frequently (23); yes, very frequently (9); no answer (6).

Question 35: *Do you use the Dutch language outside your home?*

No (16); yes, but rarely (21); yes, occasionally (55); yes, frequently (8); yes, very frequently (none).

Question 36: *To how many English newspapers and magazines do you subscribe?*

One subscription (19); two (16); three (12); four (19); five (11); 6 or more (17); none (6).

Question 37: *To how many Dutch or "Dutch Canadian" newspapers and magazines do you subscribe?*

One subscription (30); two (14); three (3); four (3); five (2); 6 or more (4); none (39); no answer (5).

Jake De Raadt, photographed beside the woodstove which he designed and built. *He has spent the past 18 years in the welding trade, building and repairing items needed by greenhouse growers in southern Essex County around Ruthven, Kingsville and Leamington. The De Raadt family lives in a century-old farmhouse north of Ruthven, just west of the hamlet of Olinda. The two De Raadt sons, Bas and John, are also trained welders who work with their father on a number of projects to improve their home. One of these projects is an all-purpose wood stove which they designed themselves and constructed over a three-year period. This stove provides sufficient heating for the entire house and has proven to be a practical and economical replacement for their oil furnace. They are planning to build a windmill to generate electricity.*

Question 38: *Asked which of books, magazines, or newspapers the individuals read, and with what frequency.*

In English: **regularly,** books (59), magazines (75), newspapers (92); **once in a while,** books (17), magazines (9), newspapers (2); **never,** books (2), magazines (0), newspapers (0).

In Dutch: **regularly,** books (7), magazines (11), newspapers (27); **once in a while,** books (32), magazines (21), newspapers (27); **never,** books (10), magazines (8), newspapers (9).

Dutch books, magazines and newspapers are available to readers through the services of their public libraries. Some of the reading habits mentioned above include reading library materials.

Question 39: *Do you listen to Dutch music and songs?*

No (20); yes, but rarely (26); yes, occasionally (35); yes, frequently (10); yes, very frequently (0); no answer (9).

Such music is available on phonograph records and sound tapes. CAANS seminars in 1978, 1979, and 1980 featured Dutch music.

Question 40: *Do you listen to Dutch broadcasts?*

No (76); yes, but rarely (13); yes, occasionally (7); yes, frequently (1); yes, very frequently (1); no answer (2).

There are no local Dutch broadcasts. It is difficult to receive Dutch shortwave local broadcasts because of reception difficulties.

Question 41: *Do you watch Dutch films?*

No (68); yes, but rarely (19); yes, occasionally (11); yes, frequently (1); yes, very frequently (1).

Question 42: *Do you eat Dutch food at your home?*

No (2); yes, but rarely (8); yes, occasionally (28); yes, frequently (38); yes, very frequently (24).

Question 43: *Are you a member of any Dutch-Canadian organizations?*

No (61); yes (39). Dutch-Canadian organizations listed were the Wooden Shoe Club (11 members) and Neerlandia (34 members). Twenty other organizations were mentioned.

Question 44 *asked for sex and age bracket.*

Male: (49). 20 or less (1); 21-30 (none); 31-40 (5); 41-50 (16); 51-65 (18); 66 and over (9).

Female: (51). 20 or less (none); 21-30 (3); 31-40 (1); 41-50 (14); 51-65 (21); 66 and over (12).

Question 45: *What is (or was) your father's occupation?*

Please be specific. (See answers to Question 46.)

Question 46: *What is your present occupation?* Please be specific. If retired, what was your occupation before retirement?

Father's occupation — Own occupation
butcher — toolmaker
real estate — landscape nurseryman grower
barber — moldmaker
bicycle repair and milk transport —
    owner of own carwash
farmer — farmer (3 times)
construction and farm worker —
    construction superintendent
butcher — senior engineering technician (civil)
farmer — housewife (7 times)
painter — tool and die-maker
self-employed mason and brick contractor —
    owner and manager of auto centre
vegetable and fruit salesman — housewife
farmer — chemist
restauranteur — welding technician
farmer — maintenance worker
millwright — sporting goods designer
bricklayer — contractor
farmer — landscaper
painter — electric-electronic technician
painter — housewife
reed and osier braider — housewife
sailor — physics professor
steelworker —
    recreation leader and nursing assistant
bookkeeper — housewife
manager of shoestore —
    grain elevator operator loading ships
bicycle shop owner — housewife
bricklayer — housewife
construction worker — housewife
farmhand — housewife
painter — receptionist and typist
plasterer — housewife
farmer — self-employed gardener
sea captain — saleslady
n.a. — self-employed (retail meat)
businessman — security man
sales representative —
    registered nurse and X-ray technician
nurseryman (international sales) —
    cable splicer at hydro company
orthopaedic shoemaker — professional librarian
tugboat owner —
    homemaker and part-time sales clerk
electrician — student
flower grower — flower grower
engineer and farmer — housewife
carpenter — housewife
painter — distillery worker
gardener — housewife and saleslady in own business
assistant resident in Netherlands East Indies —
    draftsman
architect — housewife

officer — structural engineer
farmhand — cannery worker
barber — real estate salesman
labourer — steamfitter
bus driver — bookkeeper
stone mason — florist
farmer — construction contractor
barber — registered nursing assistant
carpenter — builder
farmhand — farmer
construction labourer —
    machine designer (own business)
gardener — housewife
contractor — contractor
farmhand — housewife
bookkeeper and salesman — housewife
tulip grower — housewife
military service — homemaker
flower business — housewife
merchant — housewife
painter and paperhanger —
    painter and paperhanger
factory worker — barber
painter — interior decorator
farmer — trucking
farmer — pipefitter
highway construction worker — housewife
owner of *koffiehuis* in downtown Amsterdam —
    student and homemaker
beekeeper — housewife
tailor — tooling supervisor
director of a milk cooperative — trading
accountant and bookkeeper — homemaker
supervisor of a finance department of
    City of Rotterdam — design engineer
architect — daycare teacher
general labourer — truck driver
furniture store owner and furniture maker —
    housewife
furniture salesman — housewife and singer
self-employed businessman — housewife
supervisor in a brick factory — tool and die-maker
cattle breeder — principal of an ULO school
butcher — dental technician
diamond polisher — pipefitter
tool and die-maker — homemaker
oil-mill worker — housewife
sailor — housewife
farmer and teacher — teacher and housewife
officer in Dutch East Indian Army —
    structural engineer
peat cutter — housewife
military service Dutch East Indian Army —
    homemaker

Question 47: *How long have you been in this occupation? (Years).*

Five years or less (6); 6 to 10 years (5); 11 to 20 years (23); 21-30 years (30); 31 years and over (27); no answer (9).

Question 48: *In which of the following broad categories did your total family yearly income from all sources fall last year?*

$4,999 or less (5); $5,000-$9,999 (8); $10,000-$19,999 (9); $20,000 or more (60); no answer (12); on pension (6).

Six respondents pointed out there should be a category "on pension"; others on pension may have marked category 2 or category 3. The intention was that the monetary amount should be considered, whether the source was income from employment or a pension.

Question 49: *Marital status?*

Single (3); married to a Dutch spouse (77); married to a Canadian-born spouse (10); married to a member of another group (5); widowed, separated or divorced (5).

Question 50: *If married, where was your spouse (wife/husband) born?*

In the Netherlands (73); in Canada, of Dutch background (0); in Canada, of non-Dutch background (10); other (9). (Where? Indonesia (twice), England (three times), United States, West Germany (twice), Northern Ireland.

Question 51: *In what religion was your spouse raised?*

Hervormd (17); Roman Catholic (31); Protestant (Gereformeerd) (25); other (19); no answer (8).

Nine respondents answered "none". Other churches listed were: Christian Reformed (twice), Presbyterian, Baptist, Lutheran, Mennonite, Jewish, Anglican.

Rick Vicary and Al Santing seen in front of the Al Santing Garage display at the Old Dutch Village Market, March, 1982. *Al Santing is a prominent businessman in Windsor. He was elected alderman of Ward Five of Windsor in 1980 and reelected to this position in the municipal elections of 1982. He has served on the Windsor Public Library Board. The Santing family came to Canada from Drente in the Netherlands, and preserve their Dutch heritage.*

Question 52: *Is your spouse employed?*
No (53); yes (39). (What is her/his occupation?); not applicable (8).

Of the 53 respondents who replied "no" to this question, none refers to a spouse who is out of work. The spouses are employed as follows:
housewife (32), retired (21).

Respondents who answered "yes" listed the following occupations for their spouses:

clerk	farmer
nurse	contractor
painter, decorator	grain elevator operator
self-employed (retail meat)	librarian
	pipefitter
store owner	carpenter
teacher	clerk
welder	truck driver
tool and die-maker	gardener
superintendent	tooling supervisor
contractor	mechanical engineer
manager of tire and auto repair centre	civil engineer
	self-employed
secretary	building contractor
carpenter	male nurse
engineering technician	barber
real estate agent	
bookkeeper	

Question 53: *Do you have children?*
Yes (95); no (2); no answer (3).

Question 54: *If you had a choice, to which type of school would you send your children?*
Christian school (23); public school (49); separate school (23); no answer (5).

Question 55: *Do you prefer that your children marry a member of the same religious denomination?*
Yes (53); no preference (42); no answer (5).

Question 56: *Do you teach your children Dutch?*
Yes (32); no (63); no answer (4).

One respondent teaches her children Frisian. Another reports that her children have learned Dutch in the Netherlands during visits there.

Question 57: *Do you speak Dutch to your children?*
Yes (55); no (40); no answer (3); regional dialect (1); Frisian (1).

Question 58: *What do you think about your children's chances (educational, occupational and religious) for their future in Canada as compared with the chances which they would have had in Holland?*
Their chances are better in Canada (57); their chances are about the same (29); their chances are less in Canada (7); no answer (7).

Question 59: *Which of the following organizations are associated with your religious denomination in your area?*
Elementary education (47); higher education (15); mass media (newspapers, radio, etc.) (14); service clubs (31); welfare agencies (7); youth clubs (43); credit unions (8); labor unions (10); recreational clubs (29).

Question 60: *Thinking about your closest friends, what proportion belongs to the same religious denomination as you belong to?*
Most of them (40); some of them (46); none of them (12); no answer (2).

Question 61: *What proportion of your best friends belong to the following groups?*
Dutch immigrants: most (43); some (44); none (0).
Born Canadians: most (24); some (43); none (2).
Other groups: most (3); some (28); none (5).

Question 62: *Of how many Dutch-Canadian clubs are you a member?*
None (50); one (28); two (8); three (2); no answer (12).

Question 63: *How many of these are associated with your Church?*
Three respondents said that a Dutch-Canadian club to which they belonged was associated with their church.

Question 64: *Of how many other (non Dutch-Canadian) clubs are you a member?*
None (76); one (12); two (5); three (0); four (1); five (3); six (1); seven (2).

Question 65: *How many of these are associated with your Church?*
One (6); two (3).

Question 66: *What proportion of the congregation or parish, of which you are a member, belong to the following groups?*
Dutch immigrants: most (18); some (22); none (9).
Born Canadians: most (39); some (19); none (1).
Other groups: most (4); some (24); none (2).

Question 67: *Which of the following three possibilities do you consider to be the best in Canada?*

1. In the long run it would be best in Canada if all immigrants gave up their old ways of acting and thinking and tried to take on the Canadian way of life as quickly as they can (30).
2. In the long run it would be best in Canada if all immigrants keep their own way of acting and thinking and Canadians keep their way of acting and thinking (3).
3. In the long run it would be best in Canada if all immigrants could act and think as Canadians in some ways and if Canadians could act and think like immigrants in some ways so that eventually the differences between them would disappear (59).

No answer (8).

Several respondents added comments to this question, including:

1. I feel that (1) is correct, as long as one still keeps some of the Dutch heritage.
2. Be Canadian by all means, but don't give up your old ways of thinking and acting.
3. I would like to keep a lot of my Dutch ways, but I am a true Canadian.
4. I think (3) is correct, but the Canadians don't "act and think like immigrants."
5. I can adjust, but part of me will always remain Dutch. Each person is an individual, and you simply cannot lose your roots in your original culture.

Question 68: *In your judgment, how fair are the mass media (newspapers, radio, and TV) in their treatment of Dutch-speaking people?*

Very fair (56); somewhat fair (27); somewhat unfair (7); very unfair (1); no answer (9).

Question 69: *Have you ever faced any discrimination or ill treatment because of your national or ethnic origin?*

No (88); yes, but rarely (9); yes, sometimes (2); yes, often (1).

Question 70: *If "yes," in what areas have you faced discrimination or ill treatment?*

Respondents made the following comments:

1. In the beginning when we first came, some called us names like "D.P." (twice)
2. At school my children were often called names like "Dikehopper" and "Dirty Dutchmen" (3 times)
3. I've been called a "foreigner" (twice)
4. I've seldom been discriminated against, but I've heard comments about all immigrants as "foreigners": "You take our jobs away".
5. I've sometimes been discriminated against at work (twice)
6. I've had comments on my use of language because of my background.
7. My accent has been a problem.
8. Discrimination was much worse when we were here between 1930 and 1935. Now we never notice it any more.

Question 71: *Would you comment on what you like in particular about Canada and Canadians? Please explain.*

1. I find the Canadian-born easy to get along with.
2. Canadians give you a chance to reach your goal.
3. Canada is a big country, with space, less crowded than back home. Canadians are peace-loving people.
4. We like this huge land, where you can find everything. The summers are great. The people are helpful and friendly.
5. I like the freedom of the land. If you want to start a business, you may do so, and get ahead. It is a beautiful country, with a good climate. The people are not small-minded.
6. I like Canada's open spaces and room. I like the Canadians' efficiency in conducting meetings.
7. Food is cheaper in Canada.
8. Good people!
9. Very friendly people. Beautiful park surrounding our area. Many recreational activities.
10. You are not stuck in one job. If you want to change you have enough opportunities to do so, especially in the lower-paid jobs. Canadians accept you quickly. They let you have a lot more personal freedom. They are willing to accept you for what you can do, rather than for your status. There are great tracts of unspoiled wilderness and parks to enjoy.
11. The weather in Canada is much better than it is in Holland. There is more freedom in building and managing properties. As a person you can wear and do what you like. Many Canadians like our Dutch ways, too!
12. I like the rich backgrounds of the immigrants from different countries. Law-abiding citizens. Canada as a country has everything to offer in beauty of nature and modern cities.
13. I believe Canada is what *I* am: a country made up of persons like me, who want economic well being, social freedom, and the opportunity to express their feelings and needs publicly, and have a say in the future of Canada.
14. The people are kind, easy going, and polite. (4 times)
15. I have lived here longer than in Holland. Social stratification is not as rigid here as in Europe. I have my rights, and vote, and am equal to anyone in this land, Canada.
16. Courteous in driving. Am impressed with the harmony of the many different ethnic groups living together.
17. Opportunity and freedom, in business. (3 times)
18. Better opportunities for women. (twice)
19. Canadians are friendly and helpful, bending over backwards to make you feel welcome. They don't try to run your life.
20. No class distinction. (5 times)

Janet Krause, daughter of the Windsor Symphony's general manager Margaret Krause and Dr. Lucjan Krause, professor of physics at the University of Windsor, photographed during a visit to her home town at Christmas 1982. *She is now principal second violinist of one of the Netherlands' top three orchestras, Het Residentie Orkest of The Hague. She went to the Netherlands in 1977 after her graduation from the University of Toronto, where she obtained a bachelor's degree in music performance. She had heard of a position available in the orchestra of Arnhem in the province of Gelderland in the Netherlands. There she successfully auditioned and became a member of Arnhem's Het Gelders Orkest.*

This was the first of several positions she has held in the Netherlands. As well as being a member of Het Residentie Orkest, she plays in three chamber ensembles: a quintent formed with other musicians of Het Residentie Orkest, a piano trio in Amsterdam, and the nationally-touring Arion Ensemble, of which she is concertmaster.

21. I like the political system being free from the religion which is practised by the people in general.
22. A good country in which to live and work if you are able and willing to do a good day's work!
23. Relaxed lifestyle; few social pressures; spirited broad-mindedness.
24. Many opportunities to further your education, regardless of age. Personal freedom.
25. Free to do what I wish in Canada: Canadians encourage people to live in their own way.
26. Canadians built cities with the welfare of people in mind; there are more playgrounds, gardens, and parks.
27. When we came to Canada the people were very patient and helpful, and made us feel right at home. After working for it, we were able to buy our own farm.
28. People in Prince Edward Island and Nova Scotia are more friendly than in Ontario. It is easier to make friends there, where the people are far more interested in your well-being.
29. A very good chance to become independent in business, which we all aim for. Most Canadians are very pleasant to work with, and helpful. Social security is very good.
30. I do not see any difference between my Canadian and my Dutch friends (although Canadians are more broad-minded, which my Dutch friends here have become, too!)
31. You are not criticized when washing or shopping on Sundays.

All but six of the respondents answered the above question with comments, in Dutch or in English, expressing one or more of the observations mentioned above. Stress was placed on the personal freedom and opportunity offered by life in a multicultural society.

Question 72: *Is there something you dislike about Canada and Canadians?* If so, please explain.
1. Canada would be better off with people who are more energetic. The average Canadian is not a go-getter and tries to milk the system. Poor educational system.
2. At first the "bigness" was overwhelming, rather frightening. Canadians keep to themselves, and that is something to get used to. They don't "drop in" for visits, and have to be invited.
3. I find that Canadians are very apathetic about elections and government. They don't vote, and they don't seem to care!
4. Yes, the snow during the winter of 1981-82.
5. Increasing pollution of this beautiful country, and not enough unity to do something about it. The Canadian people are about the same as the Dutch.
6. The educational system is not as good as the one in Holland. A student who graduates from high school knows a little about everything, but has no trade.
7. Politics: the politicians often consider their votes in the upcoming elections. The well-being of the country should be their goal.
8. Secularization.
9. Sometimes the freedom goes too far. Many properties look very sloppy, because there is nobody who cares enough to look after them. They don't take enough pride in this beautiful country.
10. Too much impressed by themselves, and a very loose family life.
11. The need for more education to produce skilled workers out of young people.
12. Canadians are too passive, and not concerned enough about the world events.
13. Property taxes for the self-built house are much too high. Not enough right to make decisions concerning one's own street, one's own community. Why does Toronto have to make those decisions?
14. The bickering amongst politicians, and the subservience to the United States.
15. The lackadaisical attitude toward education, with parents taking children for vacations, two weeks and even longer, during schooltime. The apprenticeship system: if a person learns a skill in a shop or factory and it fails, he has nothing to fall back on. Each person should choose what he wishes to become, then, after good schooling, look for a job in that field. That Canada is so dependent on the U.S.A., economically, and politically. In Windsor we are even forced to accept TV blackouts of hockey games because of this.
16. Too hot, too humid summers. Too cold winters.
17. Education should be free for everyone. Social security for old people needs improvement.
18. Too many people with awfully limited knowledge about their own country, world politics, and general academic facts.
19. While I like Canada very much the people are somewhat materialistic. (3 times)
20. Canadians are nice, but they never accept you as one of their own. You stay a foreigner.
21. The interest rate being so high is hard on young couples.
22. People are not patriotic enough. Canadians often seem jealous of immigrants who do well. Most of them live "too high off the hog".
23. Not enough discipline in the high schools; the frustration of the young people not being able to get the right education for the job they would like to have.
24. Canadians seem to be colder and harder than the Dutch in many ways. There is not always the hospitality we are used to, but this depends a lot on the individual. In my eyes, Canadians do not have as good taste in clothes, nor do they care as much for their looks.

25. I find Toronto Canadians helpful and friendly. In some other cities I find the population, in general, very reserved. It differs in each locality.
26. There is a need for more religion in the public schools in Canada.
27. The labour unions are too powerful.
28. Unemployment.
29. I would like to see a stronger bond between the provinces, with one law for all. And a stronger federal government for all Canadians, including those in Quebec, with bilingualism a free choice.
30. Most Canadians seem to be apolitical, and don't know what goes on in other countries. Even cities such as Montreal and Toronto do not seem to be in the centre of international political involvements. There is not enough news of other countries in the daily newspapers, but rather Canadian and American news, with a little about other countries here and there. The only really good newsbroadcast is "Sunday Morning Magazine" on the CBC.

These 30 comments from 30 respondents represent the total number submitted in this category. Seventy others did not comment, or wrote "I have no complaints".

A group picture of participants in the Malden, the Netherlands — Malden, Canada, Exchange Visit, which took place from August 14 to August 28, 1982, when a group of Dutch visitors spent two weeks in Essex County visiting their Canadian hosts. *This international visit was instigated by Clem Klein-Lebbink, a chemical engineer from Malden Township. Several years ago while reading a book about the Battle of the Rhine during World War II, he was struck by the mention of a town called Malden, located in the Netherlands. He wrote to the officials of this small town located just south of Nijmegen, to suggest that the two Maldens be made sister townships.*

One thousand tulip bulbs soon arrived as a gift to the people of Malden Township in Essex County, as a gesture of goodwill and friendship. These were distributed to schools, public buildings of the township, and residents, to bring Dutch colour to Canadian gardens. The Dutch town of Malden invited her sister town to send an official party of delegates to the Netherlands. Thirteen Malden Township residents travelled there in 1981. In turn, 25 Dutch visitors arrived in Malden Township in the summer of 1982. Both visits were greatly enjoyed, and a close international friendship was established.

16

It Wasn't Easy

The results of the questionnaire give a detailed picture of the everyday life and history of 100 members of the Dutch Community, their families and affiliations. The interviewed persons received with hospitality yet another serious attempt to record their lifestyles and ideas.

The result is a picture of immigrants who have adjusted well to life in Essex County. They are secure and individualistic. They hold strong opinions and firm convictions. A full ninety-five percent have become Canadian citizens. They all speak English well or very well. In addition, most continue to speak Dutch in the home.

The Dutch, "industrious, thrifty, and [who] readily adapt themselves to conditions in a new country"[1], have been welcomed to Canada since the early years. This favourable stereotype has been reinforced by generations of Dutch immigrants.[2] Considering the obvious impact that the Dutch have made on Essex County, it is somewhat startling to learn how few in number they are. Their exact number was unknown until the 1981 National Census figures revealed that there are 1,260 people of Essex County, of whom 705 are in Windsor, who speak Dutch as their mother tongue. That so small a group in number can make its presence known in so many constructive ways is remarkable.

The immigration experience of the Dutch has been summed up recently by Peter Herrndorf, who was ten years old when he arrived in Winnipeg in 1924 in the dead of winter:

> We arrived and it was 40 below and nothing but white, a cold desolate day in January. I wondered where we were and what we were doing here.[3]

Today, Herrndorf, now vice-president in charge of all of the Canadian Broadcasting System's English-language television programmes, speaks for other Dutch immigrants when he says:

> I've been affected, like a lot of Canadians, by coming to Canada as an immigrant and approaching it with a sense of fascination and zeal. I really fell in love with North America. I regard myself as very much North American and very much specifically Canadian and I don't think that's a contradiction.[4]

Nor is it a contradiction that the Dutch immigrants to Essex County, in the multicultural Canada of the 1980s, still feel very Dutch.

A scene from *Jan Klaassen en Katrijn*, showing Jan and the dragon, before a backdrop representing the city of Utrecht in the Netherlands. *The puppet show of* Jan Klaassen en Katrijn *was prepared for presentation at the Second Seminar on Netherlandic Studies in 1979. That year also marked the four-hundredth anniversary of the signing of the Union of Utrecht in 1579, an event of great significance for it marked the founding of the Netherlands as a state. In honour of this event, the puppet play was set in Utrecht and the puppet stage was built according to the design of one used for many years on the market square of that city.*

Appendix 1

The Windsor Chapter of CAANS

In December 1981, the Windsor Chapter of the Canadian Association for the Advancement of Netherlandic Studies (CAANS) celebrated its tenth anniversary. The history of this organization began two years earlier, in the fall of 1969, when Professor Christopher Levenson of the English Department of Carleton University in Ottawa placed the following full-page statement in the first issue of a new journal, *Comparative Literature in Canada:*

Dutch Studies

Since as far as I know no Canadian university as yet offers courses in Dutch literature on a regular basis, no inter-university organization at present exists in Canada for sponsoring and coordinating any moves in this direction, and holdings in Dutch literature seem widely and thinly spread across Canada in public and university libraries but not in accordance with any apparent system, I should like to suggest the following steps towards the greater availability of Dutch texts and courses in Dutch literature in Canada:

(i) that a group be formed of Canadian university professors who have an interest in Dutch studies, their names to be circulated to all Arts faculties in Canada so as to encourage interest and support for programmes of Dutch studies at selected universities;

(ii) that all Dutch literary works and literary journals held in university and public libraries across Canada be catalogued and filed and distributed to group members, so as to facilitate research:

(iii) and that a newsletter be circulated regularly giving details of conferences, publications, exhibitions and lectures likely to be of special interest to students of Dutch literature and culture. Those interested are invited to write to me at the Department of English, Carleton University, Ottawa 1, Ontario.

Christopher Levenson[1]

Christopher Levenson had first come into contact with the Dutch language and literature in 1953 as a member of the relief work team that was helping to clear up after the disastrous floods in the Netherlands that year. After studying Dutch and German literature in his final year at Cambridge University

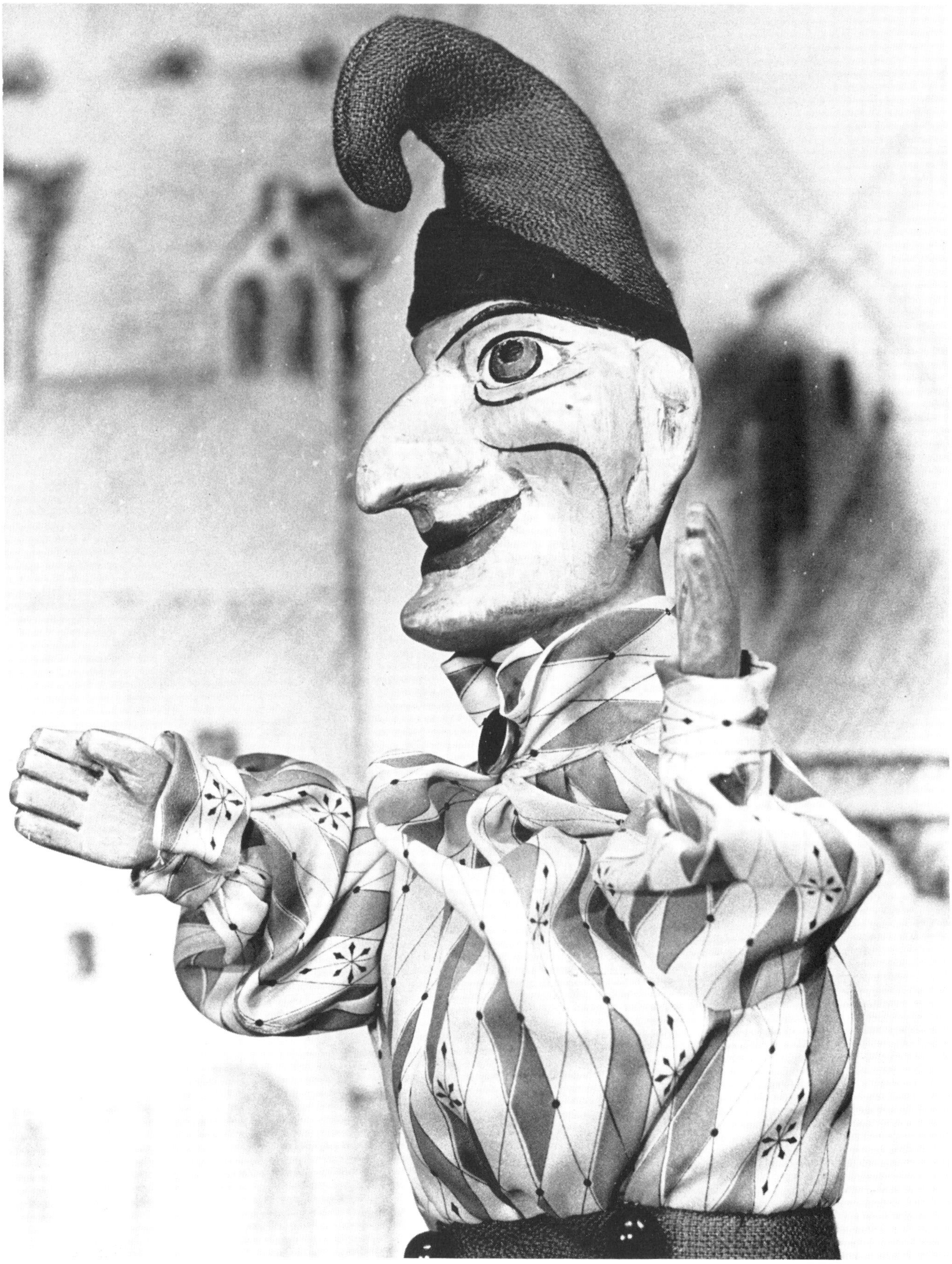

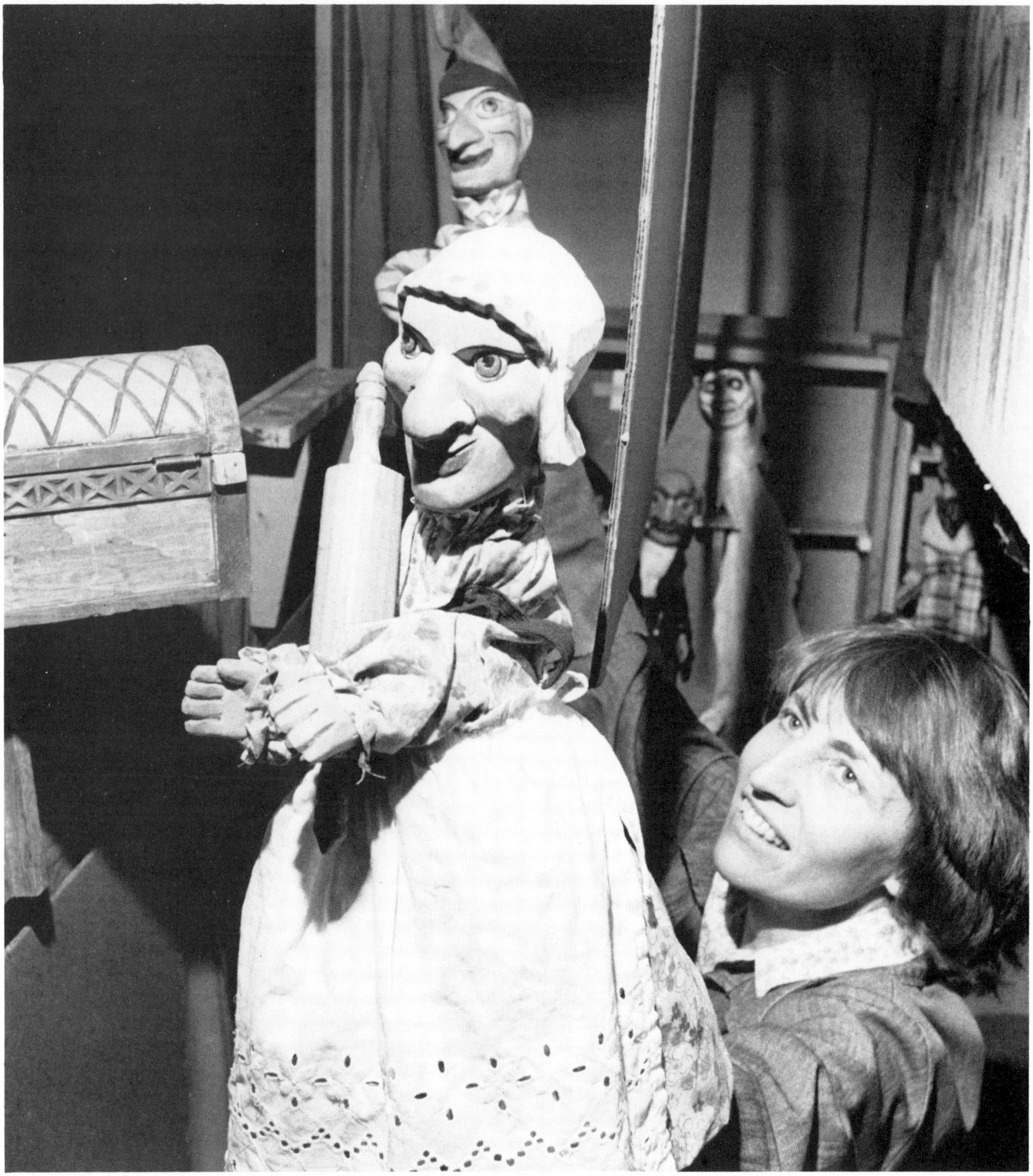

in England, he taught high school for a year in the Netherlands. Later, he studied Dutch literature at the University of Iowa, where he started a translation dissertation on seventeenth century Dutch poetry. He also had many of his translations of Dutch poetry published in books and journals. For two years he corresponded with professors in Canada and the United States who wrote to him of their interest in joining a society such as he described in the first issue of *Comparative Literature in Canada*. He asked each of them to place the following announcement on the bulletin boards of their institutions:

> If you are Dutch or Belgian by birth, or have studied in the Netherlands or Belgium, or have an interest in the Dutch language or some other professional or personal interest in The Netherlands and are in accord with our aims, maybe you should be a member of CAANS.
> These aims are:
> To stimulate, primarily in academic circles, an awareness of and in interest in, Netherlandic (Dutch and Flemish) culture;
> To encourage academic and public libraries in Canada to give substantial representation to Netherlandic literature and culture, both in the original and in translation;
> To encourage universities and other education bodies to include Netherlandic Studies in their programmes:
> To promote the inviting of Netherlandic scholars and artists to Canada;
> To act as a clearing house for the exchange of pertinent academic and cultural information;
> To maintain liaison for these purposes with other existing national and international organizations whose aims correspond with the above.
> Although organised initially through the Universities, membership of CAANS is open to anyone who is in agreement with its aims and people working in Government Departments, hospitals, secondary education or indeed any other field are most welcome to join. The normal language of communication will be English.

By June 1971, Christopher Levenson was able to announce the founding of a society to be known as The Canadian Association for the Advancement of Netherlandic Studies. From 1971 to the present, this association has held an annual meeting at a Canadian university, at the meetings of the Learned Societies of Canada.

The founding of local chapters of CAANS was encouraged from the earliest days of the Association, for it was considered one of the chief means of overcoming the problem of distance. Those members who could not attend the Annual Meeting could, it was hoped, take part in Netherlandic cultural activities at a local level. Already in 1971 groups were active in Calgary, Ottawa, and Windsor, and were in the earliest stages of development in two or three other cities. However, only the Windsor group survived through the years of discouragement, 1973-1977. Little knowing that the Windsor group was the only survivor, the Chapter continued to send sporadic annual reports to the national headquarters.

After enjoying seven years of varied and successful local activities sponsored by the Windsor Chapter of CAANS, an informal group of CAANS members and adherents in the Windsor area mounted a "CAANS (Windsor Chapter) Seminar on Netherlandic Studies" in November 1978, at the University of Windsor. This successful three-day seminar was focussed on the University community and on the Windsor community at large. The University of Waterloo had just introduced a highly successful course in Dutch language and culture, and this important fact was made the focus of a discussion on the topic "CAANS on Campus". Nineteen professors and students from the University of Windsor and other Canadian and American universities took part in this discussion which ended the three-day seminar. During this seminar a series of papers and musical performances, film showings and discussions brought the interests and activities of CAANS to the attention of all interested members of the community. Through the auspices of the Royal Netherlands Embassy, First Secretary Charles Huijbregts, arranged for the Department of Foreign Affairs of the Netherlands to provide a showing of an important feature film, just released, *Max Havelaar*. This token of support for the Seminar was a vital contribution to its success for it attracted many members of the university community.

This successful first Windsor Seminar was followed by a second in 1979 and a third in 1980. A puppet performance of a traditional Jan Klaassen show, following the text of Janus Cabalt, the famous Amsterdam puppeteer, was one of the features of the 1979 seminar. Heie Boles, the director of the Heritage Puppet Theatre, has described this event as follows:

> This production of *Jan Klaassen and Katrijn* was initiated by Joan Magee on the occasion of the Second Seminar on Netherlandic Studies sponsored by the Windsor Chapter of the Canadian Association for the Advancement of Netherlandic Studies, held at the University of Windsor in November, 1979. It was intended as both entertainment for the delegates and their families and guests, and as an attempt to produce a Jan Klaassen puppet play in the authentic folk tradition of the Netherlands. That this was made possible was due in no small part to the kindness of a Dutch puppeteer and a noted bibliographer of the publishing firm of Martinus Nijhoff in the Hague, F. van den Berg, who provided the script we needed and recommended the book *Doopceel van Jan Claeszen*, the text upon which all our work was based. Hendrika Ruger and Joan Magee translated the traditional form of the play, as printed in this book, into colloquial English. It was decided that the Windsor Chapter of the Canadian

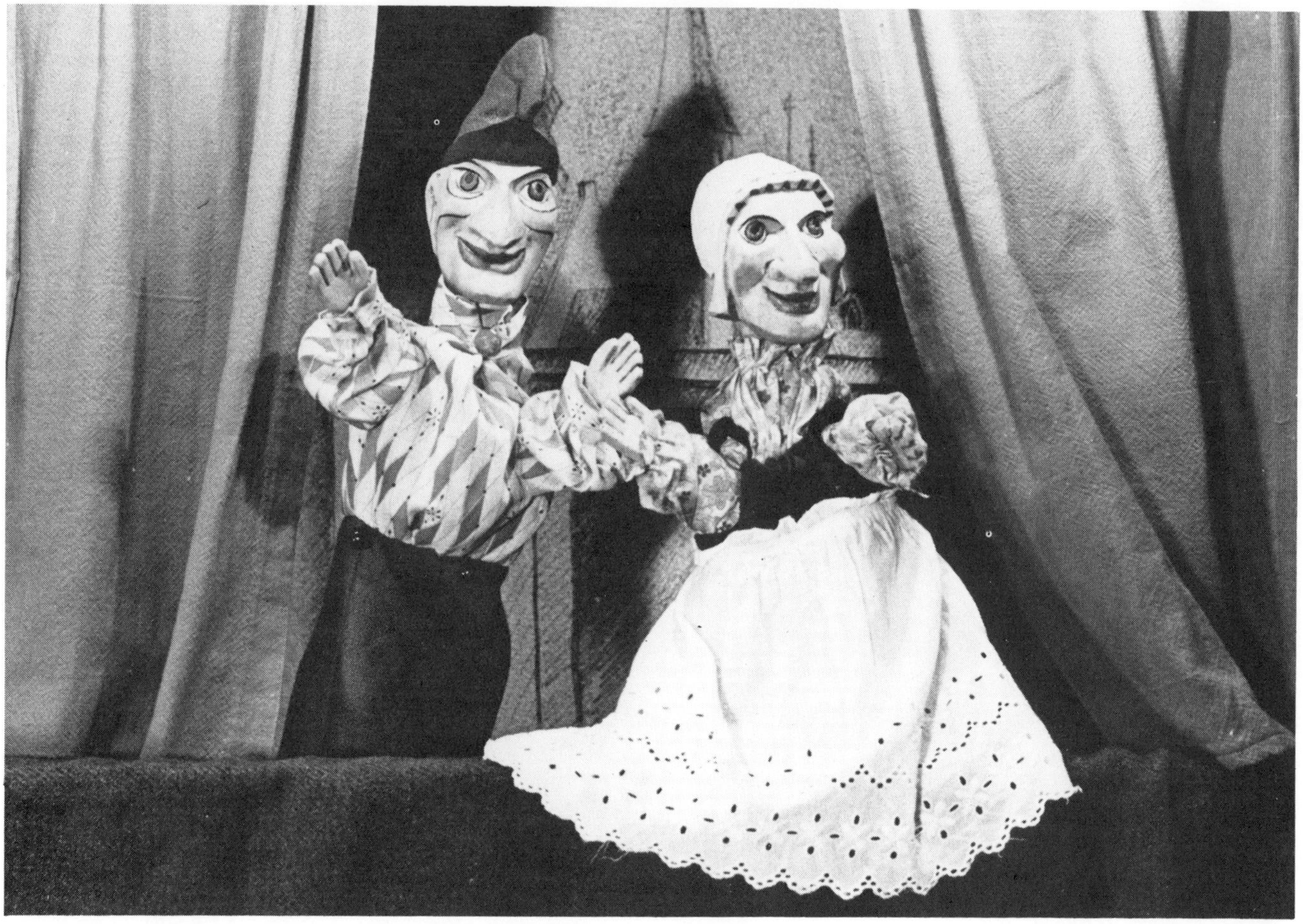

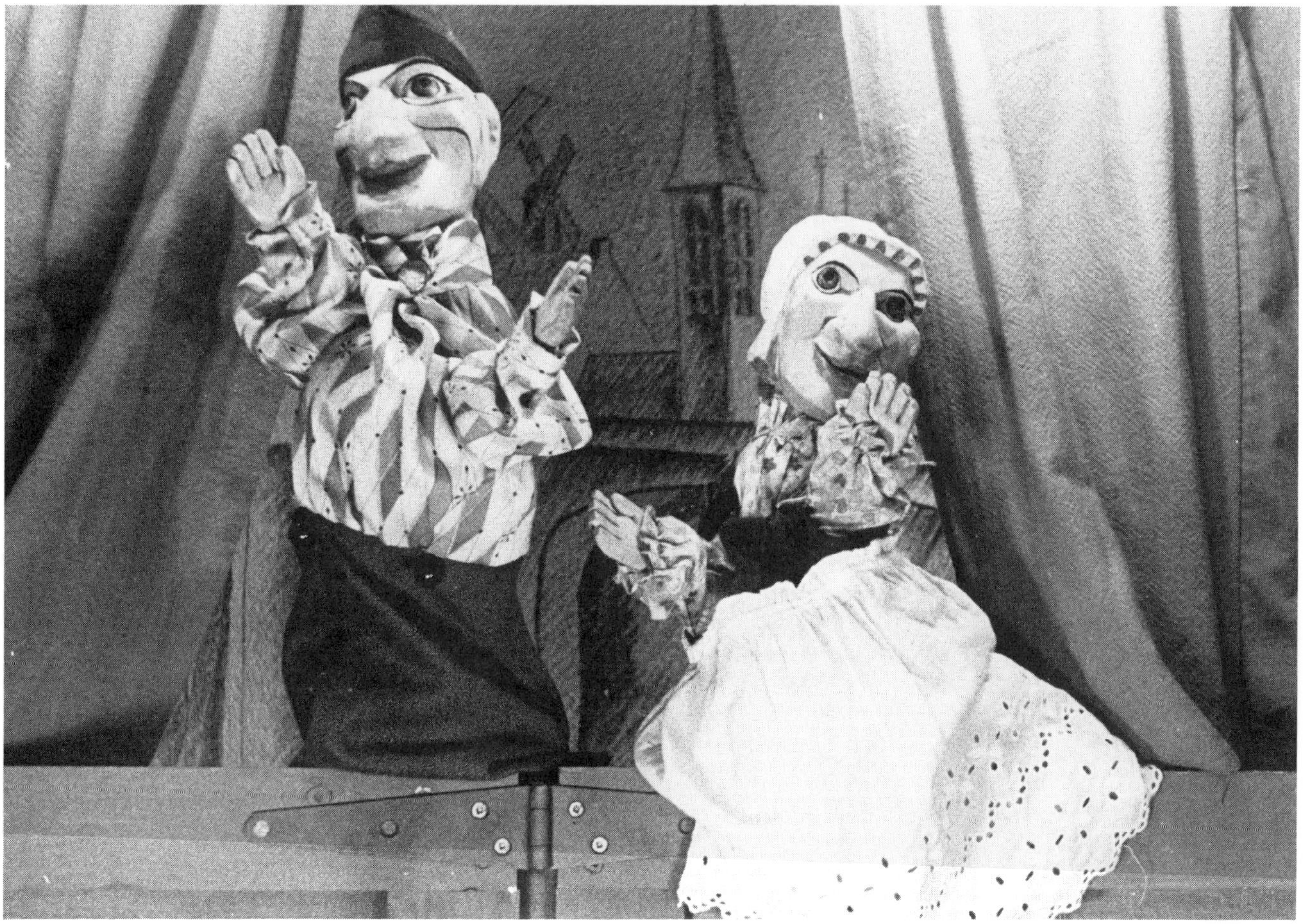

Hendrika Ruger, editor of the *Netherlandic Press* of Windsor, with some of the books published recently by this small, specialized press. *The* Netherlandic Press *was founded in 1980 and has eight publications in print as of spring, 1983. All are concerned with some aspect of Netherlandic culture, and several of them are published in a dual-language (Dutch and English) edition.*

Henny Ruger was born in Utrecht. She emigrated to Canada in 1951 and since then has lived in Windsor. In 1969 she entered the University of Windsor, and graduated in 1971. She continued her education at the University of Toronto, obtaining Master's degrees in German Literature and Library Science. In 1973-74 she did graduate studies in Dutch literature at the University of Utrecht, on a Netherlands Government Scholarship. She is a founding member of CAANS, Windsor Chapter.

Association for the Advancement of Netherlandic Studies would sponsor the seminar performance, providing one-half of the required funds of $700.00, and the rest of the amount, $350.00, would be requested as a Wintario grant. We were delighted to receive this Wintario grant from the Government of the Province of Ontario, a great encouragement for our Heritage Puppet Theatre.

After our Seminar performance, which was repeated immediately for an overflow crowd, we performed the play several times before other audiences. It was presented a number of times in Assumption High School in Windsor. A crowd of over 200 children attended a performance at the Windsor Public Library. In December, 1979, it was played for the St. Nicholaas Party of the Neerlandia Dutch Canadian Society of Windsor. Later, a videotape of the performance was made at the University of Windsor, a permanent record for the use of students of Netherlandic Studies in the course taught there by Dr. Louise Nelson.[2]

Some of the most interesting programmes held in connection with the three Seminars concerned the Netherlands in World War II, and the liberation of the country by the Canadian armed forces. In the second seminar, held in November 1979, there was a panel discussion by archivists and librarians on the topic: "Should Ethnic Documents Donated to Libraries and Archives be Kept in Local, Provincial, or National Institutions?". This topic led to an interesting discussion concerning the various ethnic archival collections in Windsor, Toronto, and Ottawa. A sample of a valuable donation used for purposes of illustration was shown to those attending the seminar. It was a fine collection of Dutch war documents collected by Kees Roozen, then owner of Mario's Restaurant in Windsor. He had brought these documents, mounted in several large scrapbooks, to Windsor when he came in the 1950s. At the end of the seminar one of the panelists, Walter Neutel, a Dutch immigrant himself, and head of the Ethnic Archives section of the Public Archives of Canada, found these documents interesting enough to take them back to Ottawa for deposit in the Public Archives. There they are available to students of the war years in the Netherlands. Among the many documents in the collection are underground items, including faked resistance publications intended to deceive the Dutch.

In addition to the three Seminars on Netherlandic Studies held in 1978, 1979, and 1980, the Windsor Chapter of CAANS had sponsored a series of lectures and films each year since 1971. In recent years, members of a similar society at The University of Michigan, the Netherlands America University League, have cooperated closely with the Windsor Chapter of CAANS. They have extended an invitation to CAANS members to attend their meetings in Ann Arbor, and frequently attended those held in Windsor.

In 1980, two members of the Windsor Chapter of CAANS, Hendrika Ruger and Joan Magee, founded the Netherlandic Press of Windsor. This non-profit venture has led to the publication of several books, some informational, some literary in nature. All of the publications of this press concern some aspect of Netherlandic studies in Canada.

This photograph shows delegates to the Third Seminar on Netherlandic Studies, sponsored by the Windsor Chapter of the Canadian Association for the Advancement of Netherlandic studies CAANS, held in November 1980 at the University of Windsor. *From left to right are: Eka Berends and M. Cusson, students of Netherlandic Studies; Eric Lugtigheid from the Multiculturalism Directorate of the Secretary of State in Ottawa; Wendy Fraser of the Leddy Library, University of Windsor; Marsha Blok, University of Waterloo; Dr. Adrian van den Hoven, President of CAANS; Ina Schepers, Hollandia News; His Excellency P.W. Jalink, Ambassador of the Netherlands to Canada; Joan Magee, Secretary of CAANS and organizer of the seminar; Paul Taverniers, Counsellor of the Embassy of Belgium, Ottawa; Mrs. P. W. Jalink; Dr. H. L. van Vierssen Trip, of Ottawa; Albert V. Mate, University Librarian at the University of Windsor; Christine Benny, a graduate student from the University of British Columbia; Dr. Louise Nelson, President of CAANS (Windsor Chapter); Julian Wigcherink, President of the Dutch Canadian Society — Neerlandia; Dr. Mervyn Franklin, President of the University of Windsor; Betsy Wigcherink, Secretary of the Dutch Canadian Society — Neerlandia; Henk Revis, First Secretary, Royal Netherlands Embassy; Ina van Vierssen Trip, of Ottawa; and Hendrika Ruger, Secretary of CAANS, (Windsor Chapter).*

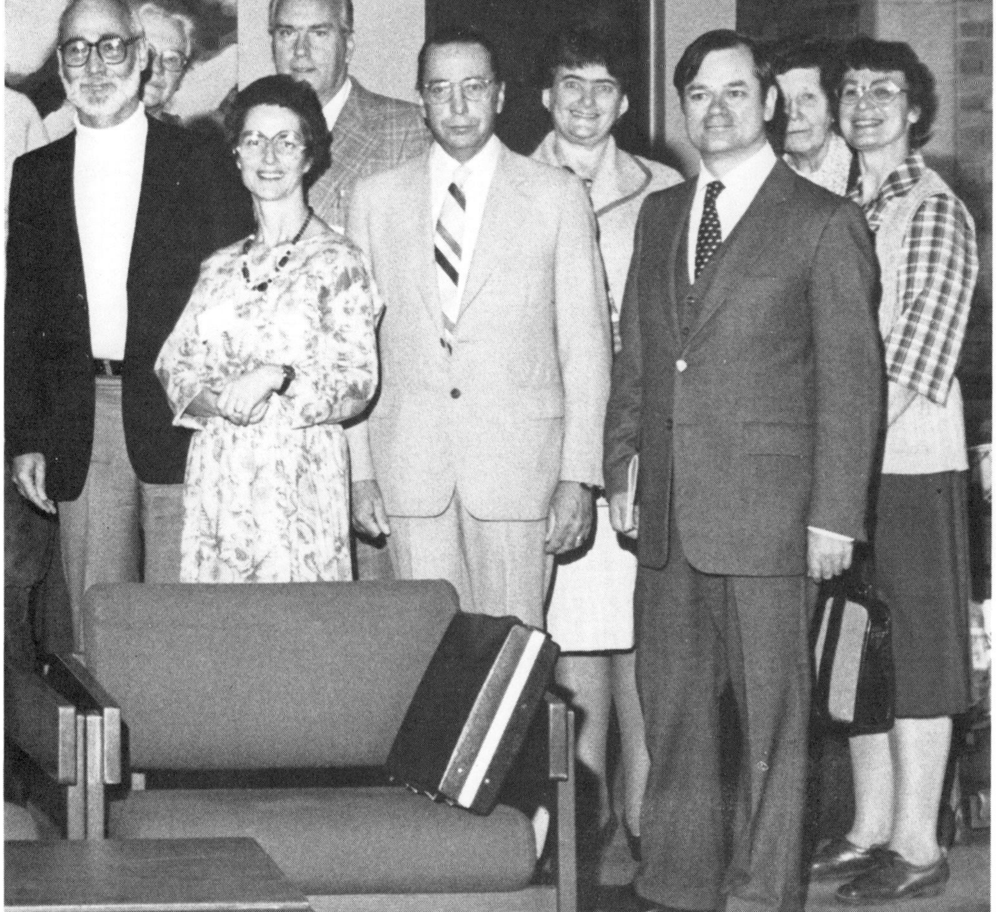

At the opening of the Third Seminar in Netherlandic Studies sponsored by the Windsor Chapter of the Canadian Association for the Advancement of Netherlandic Studies in November 1980, the governments of the Netherlands and Belgium presented gifts of books in the Dutch language for the use of students of Dutch civilization at the University of Windsor, where a course in this subject was introduced in the fall of 1980. *At the left is Dr. Louise Nelson, teacher of the course; in the centre is Paul Taverniers, Counsellor of the Embassy of Belgium; and at the right, Henk Revis, First Secretary of the Embassy of the Netherlands. The gift books provided by the Dutch and Belgian governments were a useful addition to the University of Windsor collection. Dr. Nelson has served as President of the Windsor Chapter of CAANS for the past three years, and represented this group at the Eighth Colloquium of Teachers of Netherlandic Studies at Foreign Universities held in Leuven, Belgium, in August 1982.*

Appendix 2

Canadian Population Reporting Netherlandic origin 1871-1971

	Total Population of Canada	Netherlands	
	No. ('000's)	No. ('000's)	%
1971	21,568.3	425.9	2.1
1961	18,238.2	429.7	2.4
1951	14,009.4	264.3	1.9
1941	11,506.7	212.9	1.9
1931	10,376.8	149.0	1.4
1921	8,787.9	117.5	1.3
1911	7,206.6	56.0	0.8
1901	5,371.3	33.8	0.6
1881	4,324.8	30.4	0.7
1871	3,485.8	29.7	0.9

Source: 1871-1951 Table 31, 1951 Census of Canada, Vol. 1, p. 31-1
1961-1971 Table 1, 1971 Census of Canada, Vol. 1, 3-2, p. 1-1.

Appendix 3

Population of Tri-County Area Reporting Ethnic
or Racial Origin as Netherlands 1921-1971

		1921		1931		1941
Essex County	T	102,575	T	159,780	T	174,230
	N	2,072	N	2,241	N	2,909
		2.02%		1.40%		1.67%
Kent County	T	58,796	T	62,865	T	66,346
	N	2,164	N	1,897	N	4,562
		3.68%		3.01%		6.87%
Lambton County	T	52,102	T	54,674	T	56,925
	N	914	N	998	N	1,488
		1.75%		1.82%		2.61%
		1951		1961		1971
Essex County	T	217,150	T	258,218	T	306,400
	N	3,495	N	4,539	N	4,360
		1.61%		1.76%		1.42%
Kent County	T	79,128	T	89,427	T	101,120
	N	4,403	N	6,581	N	7,040
		5.56%		7.35%		6.96%
Lambton County	T	74,960	T	102,131	T	114,315
	N	2,662	N	6,219	N	6,865
		3.55%		6.09%		6.01%

Source: Helling, p. 14.

Notes

Chapter 1
1. Sometimes innacurately translated as New Netherlands.

Chapter 2
1. There have been many boundary changes. The seven northern provinces, or Northern Netherlands, concluded the Union of Utrecht in 1579. Two years later they declared themselves independent of Spain. The Southern Netherlands, which was approximately the same area as modern Belgium, remained under Spanish domination for many more years. Spain and Austria alternately ruled the Southern Netherlands until 1795 when all of the Netherlands came under the power of the French Republic. All the provinces of Holland and Belgium were united in 1814 to form the United Kingdom of the Netherlands. This arrangement lasted until 1830 when the southern provinces broke away and formed the Kingdom of Belgium.
2. A patroon was an entrepreneur who was awarded land, with the obligation to settle 50 adult colonists on his estate within four years.
3. Michilimackinac was the name of the British fort on the site of present-day Mackinaw City, Michigan. In 1780 the Americans renamed it Fort Mackinac.
4. The former commandant, Lieutenant Governor Henry Hamilton, had taken a small force south to fight rebel colonials in the border country between what are now Indiana and Illinois. There he had been taken a prisoner, and his fate is unknown. When De Peyster arrived in Detroit in 1779 the American Revolution was well underway and there was a fear of an attack on the fort which had been in British control since the capitulation of the French in 1760.
5. *Michigan Pioneer Collection*, X, 1888, p. 540.
6. Elma E. Gray, *Wilderness Christians* (Toronto: Macmillan, 1956), pp. 70-71.
7. Frederick C. Hamil, *Valley of the Lower Thames, 1640-1850* (Toronto: University of Toronto Press, 1951), p. 349.
8. Ibid., pp. 339-340.
9. Ibid., p. 349.
10. Joseph Moore, "Journal of an Expedition to Detroit, 1793" in *Michigan Pioneer Collection*, XVII (1892), p. 649.
11. *Commemorative Biographical Record of the County of Essex, Ontario* (Toronto: J.H. Beers, 1905), p. 29.
12. John Ladell and Monica Ladell, *Inheritance: Ontario's Century Farms, Past and Present* (Toronto: Macmillan, 1979).
13. Gray, p. 79.
14. Zeisberger, II, p. 229.
15. Bruce Wilson, *As She Began: An Illustrated Introduction to Loyalist Ontario* (Toronto: Dundurn Press, 1981), p. 87.
16. Ontario. Bureau of Archives. *Seventeenth Report: Annual Report for the Year 1928* (Toronto: King's Printer, 1929), p. 186.
17. Great Britain. Colonial Office Records. Haldimand Papers, B 104, p. 323, in *Michigan Pioneer Collection*, XX, 1892, p. 21.
18. Great Britain. Colonial Office Records. Proceedings of the Land Committee, Jan. 3, 1791, Q 51-2, p. 400, in *Michigan Pioneer Collection*, XXIV, 1895, pp. 175-176.
19. "La Franche" is incorrect, as well as "Retrenche", which is found in some contemporary records. The La Tranche River was officially renamed the Thames on 16 July 1792.
20. The largest group of Rapeljes settled in Norfolk County, Ontario, where they intermarried with other families of Dutch origin.

Chapter 3
1. Hessians were soldiers from the German state of Hesse, who fought on the British side during the American Revolution.
2. While in some cases these settlers may have been recorded as Dutch because of confusion between "Dutch" and "Deutsch", some were of Dutch origin. The Malott family consistently gave their ethnic origin as Dutch in the Canadian censuses of 1861, 1871, and 1881. They were descended from Peter Mallott, "Loyalist", one of the 1788 grantees in the New Settlement. There is no reason to doubt his Dutch origin.
3. William McCormick, *A Sketch of the Western District of Upper Canada, Being the Southern Extremity of that Interesting Province* (Windsor: Essex County Historical Association, 1980), p. 22.
4. McCormick, pp. 36-37.
5. Ontario. Department of Planning and Development, *Upper Thames Valley Conservation Report*, 1952 (Toronto: B.J. Johnston, 1952), p. 29.
6. Ontario. Archives. Record Group 11, series A, no. 484. Richard Berns to Commissioner of Immigration, 2 June 1880.

Chapter 4
1. Anna Jameson, *Winter Studies and Summer Rambles* (London: Saunders and Otley, 1838), II, pp. 313-314.
2. The Huschilt family's immigrant ancestor was Cornelis van Malsen, whose career is discussed in: Henry S. Lucas, *Netherlanders in America: Dutch Immigration to the United States and Canada, 1789-1950* (Ann Arbor: University of Michigan, 1955), pp. 123-124.
3. A. van Malsen, *Achttal Brieven van mijne Kinderen uit de Kolonie Holland in Amerika met eenige Aanteekeningen en een Bijvoegd Woord* (Zwinjndrecht: privately printed, 1848).
4. "America Letters from Holland," ed. John Yzenbaard, in *Michigan History*, XXXII, no. 1, 1948, p. 41.
5. Ibid., p. 40.
6. Ibid., p. 41.

Chapter 5
1. Ontario. Archives. MU 2099, Miscellaneous Collection, 1795, no. 12, Memorandum Book of Abraham A. Rapelje, Norfolk Militia, War of 1812.
2. Sandwich *Western Herald and Farmer's Magazine*, 13 Nov. 1838, I, no. 38, p. 298.
3. Ibid.
4. Ibid., 22 May 1838, I, no. 14, p. 107.
5. Francis Cleary, "The Battle of Windsor", in Essex Historical Society, *Papers and Addresses*, II, 1915, p. 53.
6. Friend Palmer, *Early Days in Detroit* (Detroit: Hunt and June, 1906), p. 1002.
7. Sandwich *Canadian Emigrant*, 1 Dec. 1831, I, no. 3, p. 4.
8. *Western Herald and Farmer's Magazine*, III, no. 36, 2 Dec. 1840, p. 4.
9. Chatham *Journal*, 21 May 1842, I, no. 45, p. 3.
10. Ibid.
11. Sandwich *Western Herald*, 29 July 1842, V, no. 15, p. 2.
12. Palmer, pp. 354-355.
13. Charles S. Hathaway, ed., *Our Firemen ...* (Detroit: John F. Eby, 1894), pp. 238-239.
14. Ibid., p. 240.
15. Hiram Walker Historical Museum, Windsor, Ontario. Jasperson Papers.

Chapter 6
1. The Victoria Bridge.
2. The ell's length differs somewhat, depending on the country. In the Netherlands it was about 69 centimetres long.
3. An excerpt, translated by the author, from a letter published in Herbert J. Brinks, *Schrijf spoedig terug; brieven van immigranten in Amerika, 1847-1920* (s-Gravenhage: Boekencentrum, 1978), p. 16.
4. *History of Belle River, 1874-1974*, (Belle River: Tribune, 1974), p. 10.
5. Quoted in Neil F. Morrison, *Garden Gateway to Canada* (Windsor: Essex County Historical Association, 1954), p. 25.
6. This map is preserved at the Hiram Walker Historical Museum of Windsor.
7. Chatham *Weekly Planet*, 3 Sept. 1868, XVIII, no. 12, p. 1.
8. Ibid.
9. Ibid.
10. Chatham *Weekly Planet*, 10 Sept. 1868, XVIII, no. 13, p. 2.
11. Ibid.

Chapter 7
1. The British Parliament appointed a commission of five members who travelled to Canada to hear the Loyalists' claims. They were in Canada from 1785 to 1789, and heard evidence at Halifax, St. John, Quebec, and Montreal.
2. Ontario. Bureau of Archives. *Second Report: Annual Report for the Year 1904*, II (Toronto: King's Printer, 1905) pp. 1284-1285.
3. Richard Schermerhorn, "Representative Pioneer Settlers of New Netherland and Their Original Home Places", in *New York Genealogical and Biographical Record*, LXV, 1934, p. 136.
4. Mary B. Piersol, *The Records of the Van Every Family, United Empire Loyalists ...* (Toronto: T.H. Best, 1947), p. 7.
5. Ibid.
6. Ibid.
7. Ibid.
8. Ibid. McGregor van Every was named after his father's close friend, Col. Patrick McGregor.

Chapter 8
1. Peter C. Newman, *Flame of Power* (Toronto: Longmans, Green, 1959), p. 73.

Chapter 9
1. J. Maurer, *De Nederlandsche boer tegenover de Landverhuizing* (Haarlem: Privately printed, 1912), p. 20. Translated by

the author.
2. Maurer, p. 24.
3. Herman Ganzevoort, *Dutch Immigration to Canada, 1892-1940*. Ph. D. dissertation, University of Toronto, 1975, p. iv.

Chapter 10
1. Lyal Tait, *Tobacco in Canada* (Tillsonburg: Ontario Flue-cured Tobacco Growers' Marketing Board, 1968), p. 66.
2. The abundance of separate organizations providing the same service is a result of *verzuiling*. Sometimes translated as "vertical pluralism" or "pillarization", the word describes the division of activities by religious denomination. The basic columns are Protestant, Roman Catholic, and Humanist, but with many subdivisions. Non-sectarian organizations were formed as well.
In post-World War II Netherlands, *verzuiling* was a firmly fixed aspect of Dutch society: "A person may spend his entire life with very few contacts with persons and influences outside his own 'column'", as David Moberg's 1961 study pointed out. This pattern remained unchanged until the late 1960s and early 1970s, when Dutch society was to some degree "de-pillarized" (see C.P. Middendorp in *Ontzuiling, politisering, en restauratie in Nederland: de jaren 60 en 70*, (Meppel: Boom, 1979).
3. The exception was the Holland Marsh experiment.
4. Multicultural History Society of Ontario, Bel 2001. Doc. 1.
5. Christian Reformed Church. *Yearbook*, 1926, pp. 140-144.
6. Christian Reformed Church. *Yearbook*, 1927, pp. 163-164.

Chapter 11
1. B.P. Hofstede, *Thwarted Exodus: Post-War Overseas Migration from the Netherlands* (The Hague: Martinus Nijhoff, 1964), p. 18.
2. Ibid., p. 17.
3. William Petersen, *Planned Migration: The Social Determinants of the Dutch-Canadian Movement* (Berkeley: University of California Press, 1955), pp. 66-67.
4. G. Beijer et al., *Characteristics of Overseas Migrants* (The Hague: Government Printing Office, 1961), p. 28.
5. Anthony Sas, *Dutch Migration to and Settlement in Canada, 1945-1955* Ph. D. dissertation. Clark University, 1957, p. 99.
6. Most orthodox Calvinists joined the Christian Reformed Church, founded in 1857 in Western Michigan and expanded into Canada in this century. It attracted many members of the *Gereformeerde Gemeenten*, although others joined Netherlands Reformed denominations, begun in America a century before. In later years the Free Reformed Church was organized by members of the *Christelijk Gereformeerde Kerken*, also orthodox Calvinists. Those *strictly* orthodox *Gereformeerde Kerken, onderhoudende Article 31* Calvinists founded the Canadian Reformed Church.
A liberal Calvinist church, the Reformed Church in Canada, founded for members of the *Nederlands Hervormde Kerk*, was established by the Reformed Church in America (originally known as the Dutch Reformed Church, and founded in New Netherland in 1628). For a more detailed description see p.p. 14-18 of *Dutch Canadian Mosaic*, by G.W. Graaskamp.
7. Sas, p. 125.

Chapter 12
1. Joan Magee, "English for New Canadians", in *Canadian Library Association Bulletin*, IX, no. 3, Nov., 1952, pp. 83-85.
2. Robert Williams, "The Parish and the Social, Economic, and Educational Integration of Immigrants", in *Fourth International Catholic Migration Congress. Aug. 21-25, 1960. Ottawa, Canada, Report*, p. 355.
3. Ibid., p. 357.

Chapter 13
1. Graaskamp, p. 15.
2. Ibid.
3. Marty Gervais, "Putting One Face on Christianity" in the Windsor *Star*, 4 July 1981, p. C4.
4. Mark Boekelman, "Pioneer: Christian Monthly — An Immigrant Journal", in *Polyphony*, I, no. 2, Summer, 1978, pp 41-42.

Chapter 14
1. Graaskamp, pp. 24-25.
2. *Thank You Canada*, ed. Max Nord (Montreal: Stichting Wereldtentoonstelling, 1967).

Chapter 15
1. The written answers to the questions have not been altered except for some changes in spelling or syntax. Interviews were conducted in the home, confidentially, in either Dutch or English. Interviewed were Dutch immigrants randomly chosen from a 300-member file derived from membership lists of various churches, social and academic organizations having many Dutch members.
2. Questions were phrased to allow comparison between this 1982 research and that made by Joe Graumans in southwestern Ontbario a decade earlier. His work is reported in *The Role of Ethno-Religious Organizations in the Assimilation Process of Dutch Christian Reformed and Catholic Immigrants in South Western Ontario*, (M.A. Thesis), University of Windsor, 1973. The author is indebted to Joe Graumans for the wording of questions 15-19, 24-36, and 71-72.

Chapter 16
1. Canada. Department of Immigration and Colonization, *Report for the Year Ending March 31, 1925* (Ottawa: King's Printer, 1925), p. 30.
2. John W. Berry, Rudolf Kalin, and Donald M. Taylor, *Multiculturalism and Ethnic Attitudes in Canada* (Ottawa: Queen's Printer, 1976), p. 104.
3. Rick Groen, "TV Still Excites Me the Most", in *Globe and Mail*. 20 Nov. 1982, p. E1.
4. Ibid.

Appendix 1
1. Christopher Levenson, "Dutch studies" in *Comparative Literature in Canada Newsletter*, v. 1 no 1 (1969) p. 23.
2. *Jan Klaasen en Katrijn in Canada*, ed. by Joan Magee (Windsor: Netherlandic Press, 1981), pp. 46-47.

Selected Bibliography

Beijer, G. and others. *Characteristics of Overseas Migrants*. The Hague: Government Printer, 1961.

Berry, John W., Rudolf Kalin, and Donald M. Taylor. *Multiculturalism and Ethnic Attitudes in Canada*. Ottawa: Queen's Printer, 1977.

Bruce, Jean. *After the War*. Toronto: Fitzhenry and Whiteside, 1982.

De Jong, Gerald F. *The Dutch in America, 1609-1974*. Boston: Twayne, 1975.

Doezema, Linda P. *Dutch Americans: A Guide to Information Sources*. Detroit: Gale Research, 1979.

Ganzevoort, Herman. *Dutch Immigration to Canada, 1892-1940*. Ph. D. dissertation, University of Toronto, 1975.

Graaskamp, G. W. *Dutch Canadian Mosaic*. Niagara Falls: privately printed, 1981.

Graumans, Joe. *The Role of Ethno-Religious Organizations in the Assimilation Process of Dutch Christian Reformed and Catholic Immigrants in South Western Ontario*. M.A. thesis, University of Windsor, 1973.

Hartland, J. A. A. *De geschiedenis van de Nederlandse emigratie tot de tweede wereldoorlog*. 's-Gravenhage: Emigratie Dienst, 1959.

Helling, R. A. "Dutch Immigration to the Tri-country Area (Essex, Kent, and Lambton Counties, Ontario)." In *Canadian Journal of Netherlandic Studies*, III, nos. 1-2, Fall-Spring, 1982, pp. 12-15.

Hofstede, B. P. *Thwarted Exodus: Post-War Overseas Migration from the Netherlands*. The Hague: Martinus Nijhoff, 1964.

Ishwaran, K. *Family, Kinship, and Community: A Study of Dutch Canadians, a Developmental Approach*. Toronto: McGraw-Hill Ryerson, 1977.

Kaufman, David, ed. and Michiel Horn. *A Liberation Album: Canadians in the Netherlands 1944-45*. Toronto: McGraw-Hill Ryerson, 1980.

Kralt, John. "Netherlanders and the Canadian Census." In *Canadian Journal of Netherlandic Studies*, III, nos. 1-2, Fall-Spring, 1982, pp. 40-43.

Lagerway, Walter. *Neen Nederland, 'k vergeet u niet*. Baarn: Bosch and Keuning, 1982.

Lucas, Henry S. *Netherlanders in America: Dutch Immigration to the United States and Canada, 1789-1950*. Ann Arbor: University of Michigan Press, 1955.

Magee, Joan. "The Canadian Association for the Advancement of Netherlandic Studies: An Overview of the First Decade, 1971-1981." In *Canadian Journal of Netherlandic Studies*, III, nos. 1-2, Fall-Spring, 1982, pp. 3-7.

Moberg, David O. "Social Differentiation in the Netherlands". In *Social Forces*, XXXIX, no. 4, May 1961, pp. 333-337.

Nederland. Ministerie van Sociale Zaken. *Inpakken en wegwezen? Een onderzoek naar kenmerken en motieven van emigranten naar Australië, Canada en Nieuw-Zeeland*. 's-Gravenhage: Staatsdrukkerij, 1981.

O'Bryan, K. G., J. G. Reitz, and O. M. Kuplowska. *Non-official Languages: A Study in Canadian Multiculturalism*. Ottawa: Queen's Printer, 1976.

Peterson, William. *Planned Migration: The Social Determinants of the Dutch-Canadian Movement*. Berkeley: University of California Press, 1955.

Reaman, G. Elmore. *The Trail of the Black Walnut*. Rev. ed. Toronto: McClelland and Stewart, 1965.

Sas, Anthony. "Dutch Concentrations in Rural Southwestern Ontario During the Postwar Decade." In *Annals of the Association of American Geographers*, XLVIII, no. 3, September 1958, pp. 185-194.

——— *Dutch Migration to and Settlement in Canada, 1945-1955.*. Ph. D. dissertation, Clark University, 1957.

Tuinman, Abe S. *Enige aspecten van de hedendaagse migratie van Nederlanders naar Canada*. 's Gravenhage: Staatsdrukkerij, 1952.

Tuinman, A. S. "The Netherlands-Canadian Migration." In *Tijdschrift voor Economische en Sociale Geografie*, XLVII, no. 8, 1956, pp. 181-189.

Van Gingel, Aileen M. *Ethnicity in the Reformed Tradition: Dutch Calvinist Immigrants in Canada, 1946-1960*. M.A. Thesis, University of Toronto, 1982.

Wilson, Bruce. *As She Began: An Illustrated Introduction to Loyalist Ontario*. Toronto: Dundurn Press, 1981.

Photography Index and Credits

Page

Front cover picture: Jerry Schinkel selling cheese at the Old Dutch Village Market, 1983. Walter Jackson.

6 Henk De Laat demonstrating traditional way to eat salted herring at the Old Dutch Village Market, March 1983. *Windsor Star.*

10 N. J. Visscher, map of New Netherland, circa 1650. In G.M. Asher, *A Bibliographical and Historical Essay on... New Netherland...* (Amsterdam: Frederik Muller, 1854-1857).

12 Detail of an engraving, mid-seventeenth century, by G. Temini, view of Amsterdam from the formerly open IJ. Rijksmuseum Nederlands, Scheepvaart Museum, Amsterdam, the Netherlands.

13 Jan van de Velde, "Grote Markt met het stadhuis." Etching, from original painting by P. Saenredam. Rijksarchief in Noord-Holland, Haarlem.

14 Artist unknown, "A.S. De Peyster". N81 1464. King's Gallery, Liverpool, England.

16 Modern map of the Netherlands. Information and Documentation Centre for the Geography of the Netherlands, Utrecht, the Netherlands.

19 "Dalfsen: Landscape, with Kasteel Rechteren, from the Rechterensedijk". 23817. Gemeentearchief, Dalfsen, the Netherlands.

20 Typical farmhouse, Dalfsen, the Netherlands. Dalfsen Photographers.

22 Benson J. Lossing, "Dolsen's". In B.J. Lossing, *Pictorial Field Book of the War of 1812* (New York: Harper, 1868) Courtesy Hiram Walker, Historical Museum, Windsor.

23 Political boundaries 1763-1853. In Paul E. Vandall, *Atlas of Essex County* (Windsor: Essex County Historical Association, 1965) p. 27. Essex County Historical Association.

24a P.J. Lloyd, "The Revolutionary War on the New York and Pennsylvanian Frontiers". In Bruce Wilson, *As She Began*, p. 38. (Toronto: Dundurn Press, 1981).

24b P.J. Lloyd, "Loyalist Settlement in Ontario". In Bruce Wilson, *As She Began*, p. 69. (Toronto: Dundurn Press, 1981).

26 Philip John Bainbrigge, "Button Wood Tree, 18 ft in circumference in the bush near Chatham", circa 1840. C-11883. Watercolour over pencil. Public Archives of Canada.

29 Artist unknown, "View of Detroit from Great Western Terminus, in Windsor", circa 1860. Watercolour. Hiram Walker Historical Museum, Windsor, Ontario.

30 View of Utrecht, 1634. Copper engraving. Rijksarchief in Utrecht.

37 "Vanavery Store at South Woodslee". In N.F. Morrison, *Garden Gateway to Canada* (Windsor: Herald Press, 1954). Essex County Historical Association.

38 Artist unknown, "Sketch of a Portion of the Village of 'Chisholme', Otherwise Called 'Belle River' ". Hiram Walker Historical Museum, Windsor, Ontario.

45 Frederick A. Verner, "Detroit River Scene at Sunset". Watercolour. Art Gallery of Windsor.

46 "W.C. Van Horne". C8549. Public Archives of Canada.

50 Dutch immigration poster, Collection Advertising 86, date 1884. Manitoba Archives.

52a Dutch immigrants in new Assembly Hall at Canadian Railways terminal, Halifax, N.S., 1920s. C-36146. Public Archives of Canada.

52b Immigrants, Quebec City, ca.1911. PA 10256. Public Archives of Canada.

54 Hendrik and Alice Knapper, 1983. Gary Drouin.

59 William Reybroek with racing pigeons. Gary Drouin.

60 Wedding photograph of Hervé Gravel and Helena den Adel, s'Hertogenbosch, 17 November 1945. Courtesy of Helena Gravel.

63 John Fase, general manager at the Winco Engineering Company, Windsor, 1959. PA 126074. Public Archives of Canada.

65 Helga Harder examining her Mennonite family history. Gary Drouin.

66 Modern Map of Essex County. Ontario Ministry of Transportation and Communications, Toronto.

69 Joan Magee teaching New Canadians at Willistead Library, 1952. Noel Wild.

70 Sylvia Thijs selecting Dutch books from the Windsor Public Library collection of Dutch language materials. Gary Drouin.

71 Evert Van Doorn wearing wooden shoes known as *klompen* by the Dutch. *Windsor Star.*

73 Glenn Van Blommestein, a Windsor chef, preparing *bitterballen*, a Dutch specialty. *Windsor Star.*

74 John Noestheden. *Windsor Star.*

76 Rev. Peter de Jong, pastor of Faith Reformed Church in Kingsville. *Windsor Star.*

78 Rev. Adrian Jansen, director of the Holy Family Retreat House in Oxley. *Windsor Star.*

80 Rev. Jurrien Camman, minister of Riverside United Church. *Windsor Star.*

82 Rev. Vincent Van Zutphen, organizer of the Ontario Catholic Charismatic Conference held in Windsor, in July 1983. *Windsor Star.*

83 Dick Nieuwland and Herman Schinkel outside the newly established Essex County Christian School, 1976. *Windsor Star.*

84 Neerlandia — Dutch Canadian Society celebrates the traditional festival in honour of St. Nicholas. *Windsor Star.*

86 Major Jock MacLellan of the Essex Scottish Regiment joins in the dance celebrating the 25th anniversary of the liberation of the Netherlands. *Windsor Star.*

88 Neerlandia — Dutch Canadian Society celebrating its 25th anniversary, March 1982. Willy Vanaudenaerde.

89 Betsy Wigcherink, secretary of Neerlandia — Dutch Canadian Society, with the certificate announcing the gift of a quilt to H.R.H. Queen Juliana of the Netherlands. Willy Vanaudenaerde.

90 Brigitte McFadden, treasurer of Neerlandia — Dutch Canadian Society, making lace. Willy Vanaudenaerde.

91 Jenny Burridge in her Windsor home, 1983. Gary Drouin.

92 Jerry and Ruth Schinkel with Jim Barnett watching the municipal election results, November 1982. *Windsor Star.*

96 Mary Verbeek with her daughter Heidi at the PET computer terminal at Kingsville Public School. *Windsor Star.*

99 Jake De Raadt, inventor. *Windsor Star.*

102 Al Santing at the Old Dutch Village Market, 1982. Willy Vanaudenaerde.

105 Janet Krause, Windsor violinist, pursues her musical career in the Netherlands. *Windsor Star.*

108 Visitors from Malden, the Netherlands with their hosts from Malden Township in Essex County, summer 1982. Courtesy Veronica Coyle.

110 to 115 The traditional Dutch puppet play *Jan Klaassen and Katrijn* was performed at the Seminar on Netherlandic Studies, Windsor, November 1979. Gary Drouin.

116 Hendrika Ruger, editor of the Netherlandic Press, Windsor. Gary Drouin.

118 Delegates to the Third Seminar on Netherlandic Studies, Windsor, 1981. University of Windsor.

120 Louise Nelson receiving a gift of Dutch books for the use of Students of Netherlandic Studies at the University of Windsor. University of Windsor.

128 Henk De Laat selling mackerel and eels at the Old Dutch Village Market, March 1982. *Windsor Star.*

Back cover picture: Dutch immigrants. Courtesy Public Archives of Canada PA-10255. Joan Magee. Courtesy The University of Windsor.

Index

Adolphustown 44
Akkerman, Dr. O. 88
Alberta 51
Ambassador Community Church, Windsor 79
Amherstburg 43, 44
Amsterdam, Canada 51
Amsterdam, the Netherlands 12, 47
Ancaster 44
Anglican Church 61
Anne Frank (play) 85
Antwerp 28, 53, 57
Ardooie 90
Arion Ensemble 105
Armour, John S. 42
Arnhem 32, 45, 105
assimilation 104
Assomption, L' 21
Assumption High School, Windsor 117

Bainbrigge, Philip John 26
Barnett, Jim 92
Bay of Quinte 21
Beaubien, Antoine 34
Belgians see Flemings
Belgium 53, 90
Belle River 36, 38, 40, 41, 42
Benny, Christine 118
Berends, Eka 118
Bernhard, Prince of the Netherlands 72
Berns, Richard 28
Berthelet market 40
Beverwyck see Albany
Blackwell 58
Blenheim 57, 77
Blessed Sacrament Church, Chatham 57
Blok, Marsha 118
Boles, Heie 110, 112, 113, 114, 115
Boskoop 63
Bouwmeester, Rev. Bernard M. 81
bowling 87
Brazil 11
Brennan High School, Windsor 81
Brink, Dr. J. 58
British Columbia 53
British North America 12
Brouwer, Dien 128
Brouwer, Thea 86
Buffalo 34
Burridge, Jenny 91, 93
Butler, Lieut. Col. John 18
Butler's Rangers 17, 18, 21, 44

CAANS *see* Canadian Association for the Advancement of Netherlandic Studies
Caldwell, Capt. William 21
Calvin College, Grand Rapids 79
Calvinist Christian Emigration Society 56
Calvinist Emigration Society 56
Calvinists 57, 58, 62, 79, 81
Camman, Rev. Jurrien 80
Canada Southern (railway) 43, 44
Canadian Association for the Advancement of Netherlandic Studies 60, 111, 114
Canadian Association for the Advancement of Netherlandic Studies, Windsor Chapter 114, 118
Canadian Broadcasting System 109
Canadian Pacific (railway) 43, 45, 46, 47, 48

Canadian Reformed Church (Article 31) 123
Capuchins 57, 63, 77
Carleton University 111
Caroline (ship) 34
Casgrain, Dr. C. E. 42
Catholic Immigration Centre 68, 72
Catholic Women's League 68, 72
Central Emigration Foundation (of) Holland 56
Champlain (ship) 34
Charlestown 25
Chatham 21, 22, 26, 33, 34, 35, 36, 53, 64, 83
Chelsea 47
Chillicothe 21
Chisholme see Belle River
Chisom, Charles S. 40, 42
Christian Emigration Society 56
Christian Reformed Church 54, 57, 58, 64
Christian Reformed Church, Chatham 58
Christian Reformed Church, Essex 77, 79, 92
Christian Reformed Church, Leamington 79
Christian Reformed Church, Windsor 54, 58, 77
Christian schools 32, 83
citizenship 68, 94
Citizenship Association of Windsor 68
Citizenship Council of Windsor 68
Cody, Most Rev. John Christopher (Bishop) 72
Cohen, Betsy 61
Colchester 25
Comber 43
Cottam 43
Cramersburg 51
Croatian Centre 90
Cusson, M. 118
Cynthia (ship) 34

Dalfsen 17, 19, 20
Damasus, Rev. Father 57
De Bruin, Rev. H. 79
De Jong, Rev. Peter 76, 79, 81
De Laat, Hendrik 6, 85, 88, 128
Delawares (Indians) 15, 18
Delhi 57
De Peyster, Col. Arent Schuyler 14, 17, 18, 21
De Peyster, Jean 13
De Peyster, Pierre (Peter) 15
De Raadt, Bas 99
De Raadt, Jake 99
De Raadt, John 99
De Serrano, René 88
Detroit 15, 17, 18, 21, 29, 31, 34, 39, 40
Detroit River 18, 34, 43
Detroit Volunteer Fire Department 36
Dignan, Rev. R. H. 57
Dijkstra, Rev. Simon 58
discrimination 104
District of Hesse 21
Dolsen, Isaac, junior 17, 18, 22
Dolsen, Isaac, senior 17, 18
Dolsen, John 18, 22
Dolsen, Matthew (Loyalist) 17, 18, 21, 22
Dolsen, Matthew (rebel) 17, 21
Dolsen family 17, 18, 19
Dolsen's 18, 21, 22, 33

Dominion Sugar Company 53, 57, 63, 64
Donnelly, Dr. E. B. 42
Dougall, James 35, 36
Dover Township 18
Dumfries 44
Dutch Canadian Society — Neerlandia 84, 85, 87, 88, 89, 90
Dutch courses 70, 120
Dutch East Indies 28
Dutch language 15, 70, 77, 78, 85, 91, 98, 111, 116, 120
Dutch literature 70, 111, 116, 120
Dutch Reformed Church 21
Dwight, Francis 34
Dyckhuyse, Swantje 15

Ebenezer Church, Essex 81
Edam 51
Edmonton 81
Eighth Regiment of Foot (King's Liverpool Regiment) 15
Elgin County 64
Ellewoudsdijk 44
Elliott, Matthew 18
emigration *see* immigration
Emmanuel College, Toronto 81
Empire Brent (ship) 60
English language 67, 68, 69, 98
Essex (town) 43, 53, 75
Essex County 23, 25, 27, 28, 39, 43, 53, 64, 66
Essex County Council 42
Essex Militia 34
Essex North 53
Essex Scottish Regiment 86
Essex South 53
Everinghe 44
Evers, Fred 87

Faith Reformed Church, Kingsville 76, 79, 81
Fallon, Most Rev. M. F. (Bishop) 57
Farell, Lena 67
Fase, John 63
Ferguson, Edith 68
Ferry, The 31, 35, 40
Field, Daniel 17, 18
Field, Nathan 17
Field family 17
fieldmen 64
fires 36
Fisher (Visscher) family 28
Flambro East Township 44
Flambro West Township 44
Flemings 15, 53, 56, 90
Folk Gospel Ministry 81
Ford Motor Company 55, 58, 59
Fort Lernoult 17
Fort Michilimackinac 17
Fort Niagara 17
Fort Shelby 17
Foster, Frank 60
Foster, Johanna 60
Fox (Fuchs) family 27
Franklin, Dr. Mervin 118
Fraser, Wendy 118
Fredegand, Rev. Father 57
Friesland 70, 79, 91
fur trade 2

Geesteren 39
Gelders Orkest 105
Gereformeerde kerken 57, 64, 79
Gereformeerde kerken onderhoudende Art. 31 64, 79
Golden Age 11

Gordon 43
Gosfield North 27
Gosfield South 27, 76, 79
Gouda 63
Graaskamp, G. W. 85
Graham, Ansel B. 42
Grand Rapids 39, 40, 57, 58, 64, 79
Gravel, Helena 60
Gravel, Hervé 60
Gravel, Johanna *see* Johanna Foster
Great Western (ship) 32
Great Western (railway) 29, 31, 39, 43
Gregory, Francis 53
Gregory, Col. W. T. 53

Haarlem 13
Hague, The 105
Haldimand, Sir Frederick 21, 25
Halifax 52
Harder, Helga 65
Harrow 43
Hastings (ship) 36
Hawkesbury 44
Hémon, Louis 55
Heritage Puppet Theatre 110, 112, 113, 114, 115
Herrndorf, Peter 109
Hervormd kerk 57, 64
hessians 27
Hiram Walker Historical Museum 38
Hogeterp, Rev. Peter 79
Holland, Michigan 32, 39
Holland Marsh 58
Holland-Canada Association, Windsor District 87
Holy Family Retreat House, Oxley 78
Holzel, William 87, 88
Hoorn 47
Hopkins, Margery 6
Hudson, Henry 11
Hudson River Valley 11, 17
Huijbregts, Charles 114
Huis Rechteren, Dalfsen 19
Huschilt family 32

IJselmeer 25
Iler (Eiler) family 27
Illinois 32
Immaculate Conception Church, Windsor 72, 77
immigration: quota system 56
reasons for 11, 12, 21, 28, 31, 40, 49, 56, 61, 62, 63, 67, 98
sponsorship 53, 56, 57, 61, 62, 63, 64
Imperial Order of the Daughters of the Empire 67, 68
Independent Company of Grenadiers of the City of New York 15
Indonesia 70
International Christian University, Tokyo 65
Iona College, Windsor 65
Iowa 12, 32
It Wasn't Easy (film) 87

Jalink, P. W. 118
Jameson, Anna Brownell 31, 39
Jan Klaassen en Katrijn (play) 110, 112, 113, 114, 115
Jansen, Rev. Adrian 78, 81
Jansen, Peter 78, 81
Jasperson, George 34

126

Jaycocks, Maria 44
Jeveren 44
Johnston family 25
Joliet 47
Juliana, Queen of the Netherlands 87, 89
Juliana 70 (film) 87

Kampen 25
Kent (ship) 35
Kent County 53, 64
Kingsville 34, 43, 53, 87
Kingsville Public School 96
klaverjassen 85, 87
Klein-Lebbink, Clem 108
Knapper, Alice 54, 58, 64, 72, 77
Knapper, Hendrik 54, 58, 64, 72, 77
Knox College, Toronto 81
Koning, Jean 61
Koning, Rev. Tony 59, 61
Krause, Janet 105
Kwantas, Rev. Dick 79

Ladislas, Rev. Father 57
Lake Erie 21, 25, 27, 78
Lake Erie, Essex, and Detroit River (railway) 43
Lake St. Clair 28
Lambton County 64
Land Board of Hesse 25
Laurier, Sir Wilfred 49
Leamington 43, 53, 75, 87
Lemay, Theophile 18
Levenson, Christopher 111
Lever, Ben 64, 72
Lever family 72
Lewisburg 34
liberation of the Netherlands, 1945 80, 86, 87
Limburg 63
Liverpool 39, 60
London (ship) 35
Long Island 25, 33
Lossing, Benson J. 22
Loyalists *see* United Empire Loyalists
Lugtigheid, Eric 118
Lutheran Church 44

Maassen, Rev. Herman 79
McCormick, William 27
McDonald, Judge Bruce 87
Macdonald, Sir John A. 48
McFadden, Brigitte 90
McGregor, Duncan 33, 34
McGregor, Elizabeth 33
McGregor, Gregor 18
McGregor, John 33
McKee, Col. Alexander 18
MacLellan, Maj. Jock 86
McMaster University, Hamilton 81
McNiff, Patrick 18, 21, 25
Magee, Joan 68, 69, 114
Maidstone Township 43
Maidstone Township Council 42
Malden, Canada 108
Malden, the Netherlands 108
Manitoba 50
Mansuetus, Brother 57
Mario's Restaurant, Windsor 117
Marshall and Brown Company 40
Mate, Albert V. 118
Matilda 25
Maurer, J. 51, 56
Max Havelaar (film) 114
Mellegers, Rev. Peter 81
Mennonites 27, 58, 65
Meyer, Rev. W. 58
Michigan 12, 28, 32, 57

Michilimackinac 17
Middlesex County 64
Minos, H.M.S. (ship) 35
Minuit, Peter 47
Molenaar, Rev. Gerrit 79
Montreal 39
Moravians 15, 17, 18, 21
Moraviantown, Battle of 21

Napier, John 64, 72
Napoleonic Wars 11, 28
National Hotel, Detroit 36
National Library of Canada 117
Neerlandia (society) *see* Dutch Canadian Society — Neerlandia
Neerlandia, Alberta 53
Neerlandia News 87
Nelissen, Rev. Mark 63
Nelson, Dr. Louise 118, 120
Netherland Farm Families Movement 63
Netherlandic Press 116
Netherlands America University League 117
Netherlands Emigration League 56
Netherlands Migration Society 56
Neutel, Walter 117
New Amsterdam 15
New Canadians 67, 68, 69, 72
New Jersey 11, 15
New Netherland 10, 11, 12
New Settlement 21, 25
New York (state) 11, 15, 17, 24
New York Central (railway) 43
Newman, Peter C. 48
Niagara 17, 21, 43, 44
Niagara Falls 39
Nieuw Nijverdal 51, 52
Nieuwland, Dick 83
Noestheden, Hank 75
Noestheden, Helena 72
Noestheden John, senior 72, 74, 75
Noestheden, John, junior 75
North West Company 20
Northumberland County 17

occupations 95, 97, 100, 101, 103
O'Connor, Hon. John 42
Old Dutch Village Market 90
Ontario Regional Catholic Charismatic Conference, 1983 82
Ouellette, Denis 34
Ouellette, Jean Baptiste 34
Ouellette, Victor 34
Overijssel 17, 20, 32

Patriot Club of Detroit 34, 35
patroons 15
Pelee Island 28
Pennsylvania 15, 18, 24, 27
Pennsylvania Dutch 27, 28, 53, 58
People's Church, Hamilton 81
Petite Côte 18, 21
pioneer life and conditions 26, 28, 40, 43, 49, 50, 51
Pioneer Seed Company 96
Polycarp, Rev. Father 57
population statistics 11, 12, 21, 27, 28, 49, 51, 53, 55, 58, 109, 121
Port Dover 36
Poughskeepsie 44
Presbyterian Church in Canada 81
Priests of the Sacred Heart 77
Prince, Col. John 34
Prinsen, Rev. M. 81
Public Archives of Canada, Ottawa 117
Puritans 11

Quakers 18
Quebec (city) 39, 51, 52

Raleigh Township 18
Randstad 62
Rankin, Hon. Arthur 36
Rapelje, Abraham A. 33
Rapelje, Antonie Jansen de 25
Rapelje, George 25
Rapelje, Winnifred 33
Rapely, Frederick 25
Rapely, Julious (Julius) 25
Rapely (Rapelje, Rapelye) family 25
reading habits 100
Red Cross 68, 69
Reformed Church 32, 57, 79, 81
Reformed Church in America 79, 81
Residentie Orkest, the Hague 105
Reuser, Rev. Frans 72, 77
Revis, Henk 118, 120
Reybroek, William 59
Riverside Presbyterian Church, Windsor 81
Riverside United Church, Windsor 80
Robarsh, Moses *see* Capt. Moses Roberge
Roberge, Capt. Moses 42
Rochester *see* Belle River
Rochester Township 42
Rochester Township Council 42
Roman Catholic Church 32, 56, 57, 63, 77, 82
Roman Catholic Emigration Congress 56
Roman Catholic Emigration Society 56
Romeyn, Theodore 32
Roozen, Kees 117
Ros, Rev. Bernard 77
Royal Regiment of New York 25
Ruger, Hendrika 116, 117, 118
Rutgers family 64
Ruthven 43

St. Andrew's Presbyterian Church, Windsor 81
St. Clair College of Applied Arts and Technology 73
St. Louis, Kansas City and Northern (railway) 48
St. Mary's Church, Blenheim 57, 63, 77
St. Nicholas (Sinterklaas) 84, 90, 117
St. Peter's Seminary, London 81, 82
St. Simon and St. Jude Church, Belle River 77
St. Vincent de Paul Society 72
Salvation Army 51
Sandwich 18, 34
Sandwich Court House 38
Sandwich United Church, Windsor 81
Santing, Al 102
Saskatchewan 51
Scheldt River 53
Schepers, Ine 118
Schinkel, Herman 83
Schinkel, Jerry (Gerry) 92
Schinkel, Ruth 92
Schleswig-Holstein 34
Scholte, Rev. Peter 32
Schuyler, Arent 15
Schuyler, Cornelia 15
Schuyler, Philip Pietersen 15, 21
Scohary 44
Scotch Settlement 28, 35
Scratch (Kratz) family 27
Seceders 28, 32

Sensemann, Brother Gottlob 18
Shelburne 44
Snor, John 58
soccer 85
Soestdijk 72
South Africa 28
South Woodslee 36, 37, 44
Spaandonk, Hendrik 85,
Staten Island 36
Stokeley-VanCamp Company 25
Stone's Hotel, Belle River 42
Stoney Creek 81
Stratford 61
sugar industry 53, 63, 64
"swallow migration" 53, 55

Talbot Road West 43
Taverniers, Paul 120
Tecumseh Road 40, 43
Teeter, Dr. Oscar 44
Temini, G. 12
Thames, Battle of the 21
Thames River 18, 21, 22, 25
Thames (ship) 34
theatre groups 57, 85
Thijs, Sylvia 70, 91, 93
Tilbury 43
Tillsonburg 57
tobacco industry 53, 57, 78
Topley, W. J. 52
Trip, Dr. H. L. Van Vierssen 118
Trip, Ina Van Vierssen 118
Two Connected Townships in the New Settlement, Lake Erie 25, 27

United Church of Canada 81
United College, Winnipeg 80
United Empire Loyalists 15, 17, 18, 21, 22, 24, 36, 37, 38, 43, 44, 45, 53, 58
University of Michigan 117
University of Waterloo 118
University of Windsor 82
Utrecht 30, 32

Valetta Presbyterian Church 76, 79
Van Adel, Helena *see* Gravel, Helena
Van Allen, Laurens 30, 33
Van Allen, Pieter 30, 33
Van Allen, Cynthia 33
Van Allen, Daniel Ross 35, 36, 38
Van Allen, Capt. Henry 33, 34, 35, 36
Van Allen, Henry, senior 33
Van Allen, Jacob 33
Van Allen, John 33, 35
Van Allen's Mill 36, 38, 40
Van Atter family 43
Van Blommestein, Glenn 73
Van Blommestein, Tara 73
Van Buskirk family 44
Van Camp, Jacob 25
Van Camp, John 25
Van Camp, Peter 25
Van Dalfsen, Jan Gerritsen 17
Van Dalfsen family 17, 19
Van den Berg, F. 114
Van den Berg, William 79
Van den Heufel, Rev. Theophilus 57
Van den Hoven, Dr. Adrian 118
Van der Pol, Rev. Ralph 79
Van Doorn, Evert 71
Van Dyke, James 36
Van Every, David 44
Van Every, McGregor 44
Van Every, Mary 44
Van Every, Myndert Fredericks 44
Van Every, Peter 44
Van Every family 44

Van Farowe, Rev. Richard 79
Van Horn family 44
Van Horne, Cornelius Covenhoven 46, 47
Van Horne, Jan Cornelissen 47
Van Horne, Mary Richards 47
Van Horne, Sir William Cornelius 45, 46, 47, 48
Van Husen family 45
Van Iveren, Carsten 44
Van Iveren, Fredericke 44
Van Iveren, Rynier 44
Van Iveren family 44
Van Jeverden family 44
Van Kleek family 44
Van Lith, B. 58
Van Luben family 45
Van Luven family 45
Van Malsen, Cornelia 32
Van Malsen, Cornelis 32
Van Norden, Pieter Claesen 40
Van Orden, Abraham 36, 40, 41, 42
Van Orden, Elizabeth 40, 41
Van Orden, James 40, 41
Van Orden family 36, 38, 40
Van Raalte, Rev. A. C. 32, 39
Van Sickle family 44
Van Zandt, A. B. D. 44
Van Zandt, Adam Wenzel 45

Van Zutphen, Rev. Vincent 82
Vanaudenaerde, Brigitte *see* Brigitte McFadden
Vanavery, H. A. 36, 37
Vanavery family 36, 37, 44
Vancamp family 25
VanDamme family 53
Vanevery family 44
Vankleek Hill 44
Vanzandt, Norman 44
Vanzant family 44, 45
Veldhuis, Veronica 86
Vellinga, John 64
Verbeek, Heidi 96
Verbeek, Martin 96
Verbeek, Mary 96
Verhoeff, Peter Frederick 34, 35, 36
Verner, Frederick A. 45
verzuiling 123
Vicary, Rick 102
Victoria Bridge 39
Visscher, N. J. 10
Vlaanderen's Kerels 57, 85
Vriezen family 64
Vrooman family 44

Wallaceburg 53, 81
Wanneperveen 32
War of 1812 22

"war volunteers" 59
war-brides 60, 61
war-grooms 61
Warte, Die 18
Washington State 53
Waterloo County 27
Wellington County 43
Wentworth County 44
West Indian Company 11, 12, 47
West Africa 11
West Indies 11
Western Michigan 32, 56
Wigle (Weigele) family 27
Wigcherink, Betsy 87, 88, 89, 118
Wigcherink, Julian 87, 88, 118
Willcox, Mary *see* Maria Jaycocks
Willibrord, Rev. Father 57
Willistead Library, Windsor 68, 69
Willits, Elizabeth 21
Winco Engineering Company 63
Windsor 31, 34, 35, 36, 39, 68, 75
Windsor, Battle of 34, 35
Windsor Board of Education 68, 70
Windsor Castle (hotel) 36
Windsor Public Library 68, 69, 70
Windsor Public Library Board 68, 69
Windsor Salt Company 45, 48
Winnipeg 51

Wintario 117
Wisconsin 12, 32
Wonnink, Evert 39
Wooden Shoe Club 87
Woodslee 43
Woodslee United Church 81
Woodstock 64
World War I, effects of 53, 56
World War II, effects of 59, 60, 61, 62, 63, 76
Wyoming Valley 17, 18

Y.M.C.A. — Y.W.C.A. *see* Young Men's and Young Women's Christian Association
Yorkton 51
Young Men's and Young Women's Christian Association 58, 67, 77

Zeeland, Michigan 32
Zeeland, the Netherlands 32, 53, 60
Zeelandia 51
Zeeuws Vlaanderen 53
Zegerius, Rev. Hans 81
Zeisberger, David 17, 18
Zwijndrecht 32

Smoked mackerels and eels are highly praised by Henk De Laat, Vice President of Neerlandia — *Dutch Canadian Society, at the Old Dutch Village Market, March 1982. The customer is Dien Brouwer.*